The Epic
of
Gilgamesh

The Oldest Documented Story In The History Of Humankind

A NEW ADAPTATION

by **Sam Kuraishi**

METRA PRESS
CHICAGO, IL USA

THE EPIC OF GILGAMESH
THE OLDEST DOCUMENTED STORY
IN THE HISTORY OF HUMANKIND

ISBN: 147502407X
ISBN-13: 9781475024074
Library of Congress Control Number: 2012904712
CreateSpace, North Charleston, SC

Published by: Metra Press
700 W. Oakton Street
Des Plaines, Illinois, 60018 USA

Other Books by
SAM KURAISHI

Alone Under the Prairie Moon
(Chicago, Illinois, USA, Metra Press, 2007)

To my wife, Betool

*Her eyes nourish
my imagination*

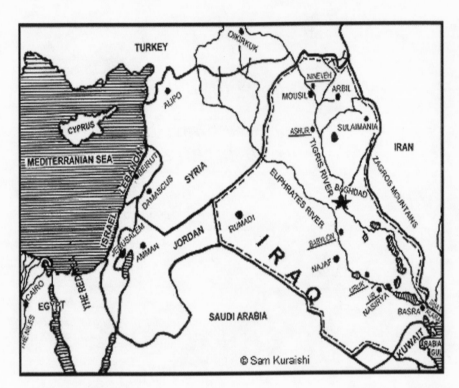

Iraq and the Middle East

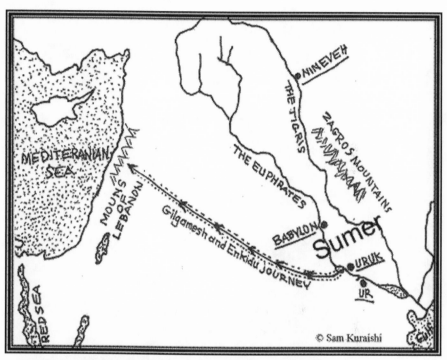

Map of the journey from Uruk to the outskirts of Mount Lebanon, along which Gilgamesh and Enkidu traveled almost one thousand miles to reach the Cedar Forest where Humbaba lived.

Archaeological site of Uruk. It was the greatest city of its time, the earliest civilized society, and the place where writing was invented.

Contents

© Sam Kuraishi

*"The love of life and the fear of death
are two famous phrases
that grow harder to understand
the more we think about them."*

— Robert Louis Stevenson

Introduction

The Oldest Written Literary Work in History

The Epic of Gilgamesh is the oldest literary composition in the history of humankind. It was written in cuneiform—the oldest writing known to civilization. The epic was inscribed in baked clay tablets that survived the passage of time for more than four thousand years, until they were discovered in 1850 and in 1853 by a young Englishman named Austin Henry Layard and his Iraqi Assyrian assistant, Hurmuzd Rassam. They found the epic buried in the ruins of King Ashurbanipal's library in Nineveh (the capital of the old Assyrian Empire).

The Epic of Gilgamesh is more than one thousand years older than Homer's *The Iliad* and *The Odyssey*. The story of the Great Flood in Tablet XI of the epic shares some similarities with the story of the Deluge in the Book of Genesis. However, the epic is more than a millennium older than the bible.

I was first introduced to the story of Gilgamesh by my history teacher in Baghdad, Iraq. He was an Iraqi Assyrian from the province of Nineveh, where the epic was first discovered. He read to me some of the passages from the epic in Arabic, which had been translated from an English version at the time by Taha Baqir, a professor of ancient Mesopotamia at the University of Baghdad and a graduate of the University of Chicago, where he had studied archeology. In 1960, Taha Baqir rewrote the epic from the original cuneiform tablets.

I was so fascinated and awestruck by the story that I decided to search for various sources to learn more about the epic. I have studied the work of many scholars and other experts and reviewed many articles and critiques from different journals. I have also found many helpful Internet sites linked to the topic.

My visits to the ruins of Uruk in southern Iraq, where *The Epic of Gilgamesh* began and ended, and my visits to the Louvre, the Berlin

Museum, the London Musium, the Oriental Institute of the University of Chicago, and the University of Pennsylvania Museum of Archaeology and Anthropology all encouraged my passion to rewrite the epic according to my own reflections and without any deviation from the thematic basis of the epic.

Civilization Began in Mesopotamia

A year after the coalition forces invaded Iraq in March 2003, the Coalition Provincial Authority handed over the sovereignty of the provinces to the Iraqi people. At the ziggurat of Ur in the Dhe Qar province in southern Iraq, a farewell ceremony was held by the Coalition Provincial Authority, the coalition forces, and members of the local Iraqi officials.

On June, 2004, Barbara Contini, the governorate coordinator of the province of Dhe Qar, gave a moving speech on the event, in which she stated:

Governors, members of the Provincial Council, sheikhs, leaders, General Stewart, General Spagniolo, General Dalzini, colleagues, successors, friends. Tonight we stand at the Ziggurat of Ur at the center of the world's first civilization. Within one hundred meters of us lie cuneiform tablets written in alphabets invented here five thousand years ago, eighty-five generations before anyone in Italy, Britain, or America began to write. A little further and we come to the oldest law court in the world and the house where Abraham was born. Here is the birthplace of civilized man, the foundation of our urban life and our philosophy.

Professor Samuel Kramer, in his book *History Begins at Sumer*, acknowledged that the origin of civilization is credited to the Sumerians. Kramer stated that Sumerian literature and poetry are still echoing in the West through the pages of the Bible.

The Sumerians were the first agrarian society, they constructed an impressive irrigation system, built cities, practiced a form of democracy, and developed the wagon wheel and the potter's wheel, but their greatest contribution to humankind was their invention of the first system of writing.

The Epic of Gilgamesh is the first written literary creation in the history of humankind. After four thousand years, we can still relate to the epic for its striking accounts of many aspects of the human condition, bright or bleak, which we still deal with in our daily lives: the fear of death, the lust for life, tyranny, and ruthlessness.

Although *The Epic of Gilgamesh* has roots in Mesopotamia, its thematic message remains relevant to modern life. The personal relations in our daily lives, the meaning of friendship, the loss of a dear friend, the pursuit of happiness, the quest for longevity, the conflict between logic and illusion—these all still occupy our minds and shape our daily lives.

When Gilgamesh revealed his grief and sorrow to Siduri, the innkeeper by the seashore, about the death of his friend Enkidu, she conferred an intelligent teaching on love and friendship, on the reality of life and death, and on immortality:

Enjoy life to the greatest limit,
go and blow your horn,
dance to the music and uplift your spirit,
you are created not to be reborn.
Make each day a feast,
take a pleasure in your food and fill your belly,
drink the best ale and be merry,
bathe in fresh water every day,
massage your body with scented oil
and herbal essence,
hug your children and make love to your wife,
enjoy the pleasure and accept the facts of life.
This is the way the human race ought to live!

This teaching of Sumerian and Babylonian moral values is comparable to some passages in the biblical Book of Ecclesiastes (9:16).

The Discovery of The Epic of Gilgamesh

Some scholars believe that *The Epic of Gilgamesh* was first transmitted verbally and passed on through many generations in various parts of ancient Mesopotamia. Some argue that it was inscribed in cuneiform writing on baked clay tablets by scribes in different times and in different

places throughout the ancient Near East. The clay tablets and other arti-
facts remained buried under the ruins in many places in Iraq and other
places in the Near East for about 2,500 years. They were waiting to be
read and enjoyed by generations to come, until an Englishman and an
Iraqi Assyrian excavated them from the mounds of Nineveh in northern
Iraq. In 1839, that young Englishman, Austin Henry Layard, traveled
to Ceylon (present-day Sri Lanka) to enlist in the British Civil Service.
He traveled by land on a road that took him to Jerusalem, Amman,
Damascus, and Iraq. After a long and hazardous journey, he visited the
city of Mosul in northern Iraq in 1840. He looked across the Tigris River
at the ancient ruins of Nineveh, the capital of the old Assyrian Empire,
and was so impressed by the sight that he abandoned his plan to go to
Ceylon. He left Iraq for a while to spend some time conducting research
on the Bukhtiyari tribe of Persia. He came back to Iraq in 1842 and was
hired by the British ambassador to Istanbul, Sir Stratford Canning, to
join an unofficial diplomatic mission.

Layard's growing fascination with the region and his determination
to explore old biblical sites motivated him to convince Canning to allow
him to help with the exploration of Nineveh. In 1844, with Canning's offi-
cial and financial assistance, Layard began the exploration in Nineveh.

From 1845 to 1847, Layard and his Iraqi Assyrian assistant, Hurmuzd
Rassam, and hundreds of local workers discovered a massive mud-brick
structure of the palace of King Ashurbanipal, the legendary king of
Assyria (668–627 BC). They discovered a treasure of artifacts, but the
most precious items they discovered were an enormous number of clay
tablets of all shapes and sizes. They did not know at the time that some of
the tablets were part of *The Epic of Gilgamesh.* Rassam, at the age of twenty,
was hired by Layard as a pay master for the workers at the excavation
site. Rassam's hard work and spirited personality impressed Layard to
hire him as his assistant in the excavation. The two men became lifetime
friends, and, when Layard took a leave of absence to return to England,
Rassam joined him.

After eighteen months of schooling at Oxford, Rassam joined
Layard on his second exploration in 1849 to 1851. In 1850, they found
thousands of baked clay tablets and fragments of tablets. The tablets
were shipped to the British Museum to be sorted and pieced together

to enable the museum to reconstruct the inscriptions and decipher them. Early in 1851, Layard halted the excavation for lack of funds and returned to England with Rassam. Layard resigned his post as the director of excavation at the British Museum. But because of his discovery, Layard became a celebrity, a distinguished author, a politician, and a successful business man.

Taking over the excavation upon Layard's resignation was Henry Rawlinson, who had spent twenty-five years in India, Afghanistan, and Persia as a soldier, translator, and researcher. His knowledge of Near Eastern languages helped him decipher, transliterate, and translate many cuneiform inscriptions that had been discovered by Layard and Rassam in Nineveh. Rawlinson returned to England on a sabbatical leave, where he devoted much of his time to examining and deciphering cuneiform tablets for the British Museum. When the British Museum earned a grant from the British Parliament for further excavation in Assyria, and with the support of Rawlinson, they dispatched Rassam to Assyria to perform further excavations. Rassam arrived in Mosul in 1852. In late 1853, after a long dispute with the French and other participants over the right to excavate in Nineveh, Rassam launched the excavation. He discovered thousands of other clay tablets and fragments of tablets at the sight of the library of King Ashurbanipal—the gifted king of old Assyria. The new discoveries were shipped to the British Museum to be sorted; among the thousands of tablets were twelve tablets recognized as *The Epic of Gilgamesh* as we know it today.

Rassam returned to England. Because of his important discovery of priceless artifacts in his native Nineveh, and with the help of his friend Henry Layard, the British government granted him a job in the diplomatic mission. Rassam became a British citizen, but his heart retained a great love for his native Assyria.

The tablets that were discovered in Nineveh by Layard and Rassam were shipped to England and delivered to the British Museum in 1854–1855. They were kept in the basement to be sorted, joined, and deciphered.

When the tablets were finally exhibited at the British Museum, George Smith was captivated by them. Smith had started as an engraver at an early age in a print shop in London. His interest in biblical narratives ignited his desire to learn more about their origin and their historical surroundings. He developed a keen interest in Assyriology and cuneiform writing, which led him to search and read anything that might broaden his knowledge on the subject. When the tablets discovered by Layard and Rassam in Nineveh were exhibited at the British Museum, Smith viewed them and studied them meticulously. With his exceptional self-taught knowledge of Assyriology, he was able to translate some of the tablets. His talent earned him a job in 1866 at the British Museum, where he began helping Henry Rawlinson sort and identify some of the tablets that had been discovered by Layard and Rassam in Nineveh. Smith came across a fragment of a tablet that puzzled him. It was a story of a great flood that was almost like the Deluge story in the Book of Genesis. However, it predated the Bible story by more than a thousand years. Startled and impressed by his finding, he placed the tablet on the table, undressed, and danced around the table, saying to himself that he was the first person to read the tablet in more than two thousand years.

In 1872, Smith delivered his finding before the newly formed Society of Biblical Archeology. His discovery received national attention, especially among those who were interested in the literal truth of the Bible and among critical researchers of the Old Testament. The *Daily Telegraph* sent him to Iraq to look for a missing fragments of the Great Flood tablet and paid his expenses in exchange for the publication rights. Smith arrived in Mosul in March 1873, and, within a few months of his excavation work in Nineveh, he found the missing fragment of the story of the Great Flood and some other fragments of *The Epic of Gilgamesh*. The British Museum commissioned him again to do more excavating at Ashurbanipal's library, but Smith ran out of luck this time. Early in 1876, he arrived in Aleppo and was not able to continue on his trip to Mosul because of an Arab uprising in the region and an outbreak of a plague. After a short stay in Aleppo, he continued his trip, but he was unable to reach Mosul because of the turmoil in the region. Smith decided to return to England, but on his way to Aleppo his health deteriorated. In a small village at the Turkish border, he collapsed. He was found there later by a British dentist who was sent to search for him. Smith was transported in a cart more than sixty miles to reach Aleppo, where he died in

August 19, 1876, at the age of thirty-six. A small pension of 150 pounds was granted by the queen for his wife and young children.

Smith's discovery and his translation of the Great Flood of *The Epic of Gilgamesh* earned him worldwide fame because of its similarity to the story of the Deluge in the Book of Genesis. Smith's discovery occurred around the age of Darwinism and Marxism and the age of science and skepticism. It was also an age of rising biblical scholars who dismissed the authenticity of the Great Flood in *The Epic of Gilgamesh*. But despite all the arguments among both believers and disbelievers, Smith's discovery captivated minds on both sides of the debate.

After Smith's death, the British Museum continued the excavation; other fragments were discovered and rejoined, which made the epic almost complete. But the credit goes to Smith for his lifetime commitment and successful accomplishment.

The Origin of The Epic of Gilgamesh

The roots of *The Epic of Gilgamesh* extend back to the land of Sumer— the cradle of civilization. The story carries the tradition and wisdom of ancient Mesopotamia and is relevant to our daily lives in its themes of friendship, the quest for fame and power, the phenomenon of life and death, the fear of aging, and the emotions that accompany all of these.

We do not know the exact date of its inception, because history was not documented during the time of the Sumerians and Babylonians as it is in modern times. The epic had been told and retold orally for generations, and, in the retelling, it underwent many changes. It was later written and rewritten, modified and edited, then disappeared into oblivion until it was discovered around the middle of the nineteenth century. The earliest version of the epic was written in a Sumerian language that was spoken in the southern part of Mesopotamia. The ancient Sumerian versions were a series of stories dating back to as early as the third dynasty of Ur (2400–2000 BC), or about four hundred years after the reign of King Gilgamesh. The early tales describe a legendary king, Gilgamesh, who ruled for 126 years during the first dynasty of Uruk (3000–2400 BC). It is possible, from what we know about the kings who ruled Mesopotamia, that there was a real King Gilgamesh. He was listed as the fifth ruler of the first dynasty of Uruk.

The Sumerian series of legends and poems about Gilgamesh were fashioned later into different narratives written in Akkadian—a Semitic language spoken in southern Mesopotamia similar to Hebrew, Aramaic, and Arabic. Many scholars believe that the development of *The Epic of Gilgamesh* was the work of scribes from the old Babylonian period (2000–1500 BC). The story was known as *Surpassing All Kings*.

The version that we know now as the "standard version" was rewritten and edited during the Middle Babylonian period (between 1400 BC and 1000 BC) by a priest named Sin-liqe-unninni who lived in Babylonia during the time. He was a learned scholar, a master scribe, and an exorcist; he was also a great poet and a philosopher. Sin-leqi-unninni exercised his poetic skill to edit and to create his version, which relied mostly on the previous Akkadian version. His version is the most complete one known today. He probably rewrote the twelfth tablet, which was not a part of the epic. The tablets that were discovered in the ruins of Ashurbanipal's library, the last great king of the neo-Assyrian Empire, were Sin-leqi-unninni's version.

Ashurbanipal was a well-versed king; according to historians, he was the only Assyrian king who learned how to read and write. He was also a scribe and could read and write cuneiform script in both Sumerian and Akkadian.

During his reign, from about 668 to 626 BC, Ashurbanipal built a great library with a vast collection of artifacts and tablets from all over Mesopotamia, and among his collections was Sin-liqe-unninni's version of *The Epic of Gilgamesh*, which was discovered in the ruins of his library during the nineteenth-century excavations in Nineveh by Layard and Rassam, and later by Smith.

Other tablets of *The Epic of Gilgamesh* were discovered in other parts of the Near East: Asia Minor, Palestine, Syria, and Iran, but may of them were either broken or incomplete; scholars are still exploring ruins at many historical sites in the Near East.

The fascination with *The Epic of Gilgamesh* for its parallel to some biblical stories and for its significance as the oldest literary composition in the history of humankind inspired many Assyriology and biblical scholars to search for more tablets throughout the Near East and other historical locations. We hope that one day their search will be materialized and we can enjoy *The Epic of Gilgamesh* in its fullest.

The Setting of the Epic

The story begins and ends in the city-state of Uruk on the east side of the Euphrates River. Uruk was the majestic home of the legendary King Gilgamesh. My last visit to the ruins of Uruk inspired my obsession about its mystique and led me to delve into its past.

After Iraq embraced Islam, Uruk became known as Al-Warkaa. The archeological site of this ancient place is about 150 miles south of Baghdad, the capital of Iraq. Driving near the ruins of Uruk, visitors can spot some reed houses around the marshes of southern Iraq that resemble the houses mentioned in old Sumerian stories and tales. Conceivably, the old Sumerians are the ancestors of the inhabitants of these houses.

Around 5000BC, Uruk was inhabited continuously until the fifth century AD; at its peak, Uruk was a well-organized city, socially and culturally, with over fifty thousand inhabitants. It was the first and largest urban city in the world at the time. The Bible refers to Uruk in the Book of Genesis as Erech. Tracing the remnants of the city wall, recent excavators have speculated that it extended six miles around the city and buttressed more than nine hundred towers.

When it comes to history, we are aware that there is a gap between myth and reality. It became known from legends and tales that were uncovered by archeologists that the massive wall around Uruk was built around 2700 BC by King Gilgamesh. He may have been a legendary king, but his city is real enough to favor the setting of his story.

Gilgamesh, undisputed ruler of Uruk and protector of his city, was known as an arrogant king who could have anything he desired. When the citizens of Uruk complained to the gods to create a match for him to offset his power, the gods listened to their complaint and created Enkidu. While Gilgamesh was a man of cultural urban life, Enkidu was a man of the wild. These two personalities and their settings made for a riveting story.

How far was the wilderness from the civilized city-state of Uruk? The wilderness, as it was known, extended beyond the settlement outside the wall of the city. Settlers around the city wall and beyond were herders and farmers; their land was suited for growing grains and planting orchards. There were plenty of date palms and grazing pastures that extended beyond the wall of the city. In addition to practicing agriculture, many settlers hunted in the wilderness, where abundant wildlife roamed.

The setting of the story moved from the city to the untamed wilderness, where Enkidu lived. He knew of nothing that existed beyond the wilderness; his only companions were the animals of the wild. He grazed and drank with them, and he protected them from hunters and trappers. He lived in harmony with all the creatures of the wild and their habitat, and knew nothing about the civilization of his time.

A trapper who moved between the city and the wilderness spotted Enkidu at a watering hole drinking with the animals of the wild. The trapper was frightened by the mighty physique and the bewildering appearance of this naked, hairy man.

The trapper rushed back to tell his father about what he saw. His father advised him to go to Uruk and describe what he had seen to Gilgamesh. After telling his story to Gilgamesh, the trapper was counseled by Gilgamesh to go to the temple of Ishtar and take with him an experienced seducer to the wilderness to tame the wild creature. The trapper took Shamhat the harlot with him and returned to the wilderness.

In the wilderness, the trapper and Shamhat waited for Enkidu to come to the watering hole to drink with the wild animals. When Shamhat saw Enkidu, she stripped naked, lay on her back, and spread her legs to show Enkidu her beauty. When Enkidu saw her, he rushed toward her and made love to her over and over for six days and seven nights. Afterward, he tried to rejoin the herd, but the herd rejected him. So he decided to go back to Shamhat. She accomplished her mission to seduce Enkidu and persuade him to abandon the wilderness and accompany her to the civilized world. She dressed him and brought him to the shepherd's settlement, where he was welcomed by the settlers. They were impressed by his mighty build and his unusual strength. They welcomed him with exuberance. They trimmed his hairy body, massaged his skin with scented oil, dressed him like a warrior, and made him a civilized man. They taught him how to eat bread and drink ale, which he had never had before. They trusted him to be their night guard and their shepherd boy.

While Enkidu was making love to Shamhat, he saw a passerby rushing toward Uruk. Shamhat learned from the passerby that he was invited to a wedding banquet where contract marriages were held. Enkidu was outraged when he learned that King Gilgamesh claimed the right to sleep with the bride before the bridegroom does. Enkidu demanded that Shamhat take him to Uruk to challenge Gilgamesh and to block him from entering the bride's bedroom. Soon after, the setting follows the path to the city, where Enkidu confronts Gilgamesh.

Seeing Enkidu entering Uruk, the people in the town square gathered around him in admiration. They were aroused and awestruck by the bulk of his body and thought of him as the one who could be the right match for Gilgamesh. When Enkidu saw Gilgamesh leading the procession toward the new bride's bedroom, he forcefully blocked Gilgamesh and stopped him from entering the room. The two fought fiercely all day. Their continuous stumbling caused walls to crack and doors to smash. Gilgamesh eventually overpowered Enkidu, and the fight ended. Enkidu acknowledged the ability of Gilgamesh to withstand his challenge. They ended the fight, hugged each other, and became inseparable friends.

The setting then moves from the city to the wilderness in a long journey for Gilgamesh and Enkidu to the Cedar Forest of Lebanon. Their intent is to kill Humbaba and to cut the tallest cedar tree to build a monumental door for the temple of Eanna.

After an extensive preparation for their long and risky journey to invade the Cedar Forest, they marched to the plaza loaded with weapons. Young and old crowded the street to offer their blessing for their king and to wish him a safe return to his homeland. The journey was to take them almost one thousand miles to reach the Cedar Forest, which is almost the distance to Mount Lebanon.

They crossed desert lands and passed through dangerous hills and mountains to reach the Cedar Forest.

After walking sixty miles from Uruk, they stopped to eat. After walking another ninety miles, they camped for the night near a mountain. Gilgamesh climbed the nearby mountain and spread a holy flour for the sun god Shamash as an offering to confer him with a pleasant dream. Enkidu built a shelter for Gilgamesh to sleep in and to protect him from the unpredictable weather. Enkidu performed a ritual for Gilgamesh and wished him a pleasant dream. After five dreadful dreams in five nights, which frightened Gilgamesh, Enkidu assured Gilgamesh that all his dreams were good omens. In these five days, they had walked over nine hundred miles and were within ninety miles of the outskirts of the Cedar Forest. Mount Lebanon was visible from that distance. They were amazed by the dense green color of the enchanted forest and the sweet scent of the cedar trees. As they reached the entrance to the forest, Enkidu was hesitant to enter the forest, because he knew that Humbaba would guard and protect the forest viciously and mercilessly. But Gilgamesh encouraged him to draw his weapons and challenge Humbaba. Humbaba, with his sharp hearing, heard the stomping of their feet from a far distance and was ready to confront them.

Humbaba warned Gilgamesh not to listen to Enkidu. Gilgamesh was too cautious to draw his weapons to attack Humbaba. Enkidu told his friend to pay no attention to Humbaba's words and encouraged Gilgamesh to get ready to draw his weapons and attack Humbaba.

Shamash came to the aid of Gilgamesh and Enkidu by sending thirteen violent storms from all directions that struck Humbaba and sent him staggering to the ground. Humbaba begged Gilgamesh to save his life; in exchange, he offered to let Gilgamesh chop down any tree he wished. But Enkidu urged his friend to kill Humbaba quickly, before the gods find out. When Humbaba heard these words, he put a curse on Enkidu.

Gilgamesh struck Humbaba's neck, severed it, and saved the head as a trophy for the people of Uruk. Gilgamesh and Enkidu cut the tallest cedar and drifted with it along the mighty Euphrates River back to Uruk with Humbaba's head.

The setting now goes back to Uruk, where the citizens were awaiting their hero. At the end of their long journey, Gilgamesh took off his blood-soiled clothing, washed himself, rubbed his body with scented oil, groomed his hair, and wore his royal attire. When goddess Ishtar looked at him, she was captivated by his looks. She promised him things that no man could ever possess if he would become her lover.

Gilgamesh rejected Ishtar's promises and sexual advances. He reminded her of the way she treated all her ex-lovers and of the way she inflicted sorrow and agony upon them.

Ishtar became so agitated from Gilgamesh's accusation that she begged her father, Anu, father of the gods, to let her have the Bull of Heaven to punish Gilgamesh and to bring havoc to his people. After some discussion, Anu agreed to let Ishtar have the Bull of Heaven. She took the bull by the nose ring and descended with it to Uruk.

The setting returns to Uruk, where the Bull of Heaven violently attacks and kills the people and destroys their land. His unstoppable rage dried the marshes and burned the reeds, destroyed the crops and blew them in all directions, and cracked the earth wide open. The bull's first snort opened a deep pit, where one hundred people died; his second snort opened a deeper pit, where two hundred people died; and his third snort opened another pit, into which Enkidu fell. But Enkidu escaped from the pit and began chasing the Bull of Heaven. He held the Bull of Heaven by the tail and called for Gilgamesh to come to his aid. Gilgamesh pulled his sword and struck the Bull of Heaven by the neck, cut his abdomen open, pulled out his heart, and offered it to Shamash as sacrifice. After kneeling before Shamash, Gilgamesh and Enkidu went to the Euphrates River, where they washed themselves, embraced each other, and headed for the city center, where people gathered to greet them. In Uruk, citizens of all ages blessed their heroes for saving them from the devastation inflicted upon them by the Bull of Heaven. But these joyful events didn't last long.

After having two frightening dreams, Enkidu felt that death was descending upon him. Enkidu started to feel pain all over his body and knew that his end was near. Within twelve days, Enkidu's health deteriorated. He grieved about dying in bed instead of dying in battle as a warrior and a hero.

Gilgamesh never left his dying friend's bedside. Gilgamesh veiled his dearest friend's face and began to sigh and cry and reminisce about the great times and the risky adventures they shared. Soon after Enkidu's death, Gilgamesh eulogized his dearest friend and ordered a mourning period in all the land. Then he ripped off his royal garments as if they were a curse, pulled out his hair, and discarded it in a stirring outrage.

Fearing his own death, Gilgamesh could not accept the reality of his own demise. He set himself for a perilous journey—defying all the odds—in search of immortality.

The setting switches from Uruk to the wilderness and into the forbidden land and beyond. Gilgamesh leaves his city in search of his ancestor Utanapishtim, who survived the Great Flood and who was granted an eternal life by the gods. After many days of traveling in the wilderness, Gilgamesh rested near a mountain pass. He was frightened by the thunderous echo of roaring lions. Before he went to sleep, Gilgamesh appealed to the moon god Sin to give him courage and protect him from danger. After arousing from a dream, Gilgamesh drew his ax and chased the lions, slew them, ate their meat, and wore their skin. After days of wandering in the wilderness, Gilgamesh arrived near the twin peak of Mount Mashu, where the sun sets and rises. The mountain was guarded by scorpion creatures that never let anyone pass through the path of the sun. The scorpion creatures warned Gilgamesh about the hazard he will encounter on the path, but Gilgamesh insisted that he must travel through the passage of the sun to get to Utanapishtim.

Because the scorpion creatures see in Gilgamesh a divine man, they let him enter the path. As Gilgamesh enters, an absolute darkness envelops the path, and he cannot see anything in front of him or behind him. He traveled over seventy-two miles in absolute darkness to reach the end of the sun path. When Gilgamesh reached the end of the path, he felt a gentle breeze cooling his face. He was captivated by the beauty of a bright dawn lighting an enchanted garden of precious trees: carnelian trees bearing clusters of grapes, lapis lazuli trees bearing bright leaves, ruby trees, emerald trees, turquoise trees, and amber trees. This was the garden of the gods mentioned in many holy books with trees of paradise: palm trees, olive trees, and fig trees.

Gilgamesh found an inn by the seashore on the far side of the garden. Siduri, the quick-witted innkeeper, was wary of the strange-looking man. She wanted to know who he was and what he was looking for. Gilgamesh expressed his fear of death to the innkeeper and appealed to her to show him the way to Utanapishtim, the faraway. She expressed sympathy for what had happened to his friend and gave him intelligent advice on life and death. She advised him to find Urshanabi, Utanapishtim's ferryman, who knew the passageway to Utanapishtim. But she warned him about the risk he would encounter on the treacherous journey and about the danger he would face when crossing the Waters of Death.

Gilgamesh rushed to the forest in an outrage, smashed the magical stones with his ax, and threw them in the river. When Urshanabi saw Gilgamesh smashing the stones, he tried to stop him, but it was too late. Gilgamesh told Urshanabi about himself and about his journey to seek Utanapishtim. Urshanabi told Gilgamesh that no one can cross the Waters of Death without the magical stones. He demanded that Gilgamesh go to the forest and cut three hundred thrusting poles. Gilgamesh went to the forest and cut the poles and loaded them into the boat. They began their voyage and encountered no hazards. When they reached the Waters of Death, Urshanabi warned Gilgamesh about the danger ahead and told him to use the poles to push the ferry and not to let his hands touch the dangerous water. They made it through the Waters of Death; the danger was behind them, and the way to Utanapishtim's faraway land was ahead of them. Using Gilgamesh's clothes as sails, the two men let the winds glide them to Utanapishtim's shore.

When Gilgamesh went ashore, Utanapishtim began to question him. Heaving a sigh, Gilgamesh told Utanapishtim about his fear of death after his friend Enkidu died.

Gilgamesh was bemused by the human look of Utanapishtim. Gilgamesh had thought that Utanapishtim was a godlike, supernatural being; he asked him how he was granted an eternal life and how he had survived the Great Flood. Utanapishtim told Gilgamesh the whole story about the Deluge, how he survived it, and how he was granted eternity. He advised Gilgamesh to be satisfied with what he possesses and what he expects from life.

Utanapishtim revealed to Gilgamesh the mystery of eternal life: eternal life is granted only for the gods and by the gods. He advised Gilgamesh to go back to his homeland and accept the facts of life and be satisfied with what he is. But he gave Gilgamesh an alternative: a test, after which, if he passed, he could be granted eternal life by the gods.

The test was for Gilgamesh to stay awake for seven nights. If Gilgamesh could pass that test, then Utanapishtim could find a way to help him. But Gilgamesh failed the test and lost all hope in his quest for eternity. Utanapishtim ordered Urshanabi, the ferryman, to wash Gilgamesh, dress him like a king, and leave with him and never come back to his shores. Utanapishtim's wife suggested that Gilgamesh, after a long and a dreadful journey, should not go back to his homeland empty-handed. Utanapishtim revealed to Gilgamesh a secret that only the gods know. He showed him where to find a plant under the sea that can bestow a renewal of life.

Gilgamesh left Utanapishtim's shores and found where the plant grows. With stones wrapped around his feet, Gilgamesh dived down to the bottom of the sea and obtained the plant. He stopped to bathe in a lagoon, and while he was bathing, a snake ate the plant. The snake sloughed its skin and rejuvenated its life. Everything Gilgamesh was hoping for was now gone. After all that long and hopeful journey to the end of the world, Gilgamesh came home without any hope of finding a way to live forever.

Acknowledging Utanapishtim's guidance and Siduri's advice on life and death, Gilgamesh became knowledgeable and wise. He realized that his life on earth is limited, and the only everlasting memory he can leave is his accomplishments. After giving up all hope of finding the mystery of life and death, Gilgamesh returned to Uruk with Urshanabi, the ferryman. The story ends where it began: in Uruk.

Showing the fortified city of Uruk, its massive wall, and its great expanse to Urshanabi, Gilgamesh realized that his remarkable achievement will be his eternal monument, which will endure the passage of time.

Characters in The Epic of Gilgamesh

There are major characters and minor characters in the epic. Each character plays an impressive role, which makes the story interesting and powerful.

GILGAMESH:

A legendary and unchallenged king of the great city of Uruk. It is possible that there was a real King Gilgamesh who ruled Uruk. As far as we know from sources uncovered by many scholars, a historical King Gilgamesh was listed with the kings who ruled Mesopotamia during the first dynasty of Uruk (3000–2400 BC). Gilgamesh was listed as the fifth ruler, who reigned for 126 years. He was a godlike man of unmatched strength—son of the divine King Lugalbanda, offspring of cow goddess Ninsun, by virtue of whom he was two-thirds divine, one-third man. He was the most powerful and the most handsome man of his time.

Both feared and loved by his subjects, Gilgamesh exercised the absolute power of a leader who can have anything he desires: sleeping with any bride before the bridegroom does, exploiting forced labor, and defying his people on any advice or suggestion that might harm him or his subjects. He insists on his ability as a leader in charge of any venture that substantiates his reputation as a supreme leader. After the death of Enkidu, his dearest friend and companion, Gilgamesh became depressed and started to fear his own destiny. He journeyed to the end of the world in search of the secret of immortality. After a long and dangerous quest, he returned to his beloved Uruk and became unselfish and wise. He realized that life has limitations. He acknowledged his accomplishment: the great wall, the fortified city, and Eanna's monumental temple, as his eternal monument.

ENKIDU:

The tyranny and oppression Gilgamesh inflicted upon his citizens caused them to complain to the gods to create a match to offset Gilgamesh's mighty power. In response, the gods directed mother goddess Aruru, creator of humankind, to create an equal to mighty Gilgamesh. Aruru created Enkidu from a pinch of clay and tossed it into the wilderness, where it grew into a powerful man with hair all over his body. He roamed the wilderness, grazed with the animals of the wild, drank water with them, and protected them from the hunter-trappers—the epitome of uncivilized man.

There is a parallel between the creation of Enkidu and Adam—they were not created by a man and woman. Enkidu was created from a pinch of clay; Adam, according to the Old Testament, was created from "the dust of the ground." They both grew up in the wilderness. Enkidu grew up in the wilderness of southern Mesopotamia (southern Iraq); Adam was raised in the Garden of Eden—also claimed to be in southern Mesopotamia.

A hunter-trapper spotted Enkidu at a watering hole drinking with the animals of the wild. Frightened by Enkidu's appearance, the trapper rushed back to his father and told him about the wild creature he saw. His father advised him to go to Gilgamesh and tell him the whole story. Hearing the description of this wild creature, Gilgamesh demanded that the trapper go to the temple of Eanna and seek Shamhat, the priestess prostitute who knows the art of seducing men. The trapper led Shamhat to the wilderness and waited for Enkidu near the watering hole. As Enkidu approached the watering hole with the herd, Shamhat stripped naked and laid on her back—the first time Enkidu saw a human. He drew closer to her and started to make love to her; the love making continued for six days and seven nights. Enkidu tried to rejoin the wild animals, but the animals turned away from him. He went back to Shamhat. She decided to take Enkidu to Uruk to civilize him. At a shepherd's village, she introduced him to human food and taught him how to eat it. She made a civilized man out of him and suggested that he should go to Uruk, see the civilized world, and meet Gilgamesh.

In Uruk, a challenge and a confrontation started between Gilgamesh and Enkidu; at the end of the fight, Enkidu acknowledged Gilgamesh's superiority. They finally embraced each other and became lifelong friends.

A few scholars have hinted that the relationship between Gilgamesh and Enkidu is a homosexual one. But to judge the moral values of any society, a person must be, in one way or another, a part of the social structure or exist within its frame for a period of time. Information and/or evidence gathered by some scholars that could be speculation or an inconsistent interpretation might be accepted by some as fact. Having lived for a time in Iraq, I experienced some of the social values that may have been inherited from old Mesopotamia: men kissing cheeks in public, holding hands in the streets, and calling each other "my love" (*habibi* in Arabic or *mukhibba* in Assyrian). The words Gilgamesh uses to reflect his love toward his dearest friend Enkidu are mostly symbols and metaphor—most Semitic languages, especially poetry, are full of similes, symbols, and metaphors.

THE HUNTER-TRAPPER:

A minor character in the epic, the hunter-trapper discovered Enkidu grazing with wild animals. He rushed to his father and told him about how Enkidu destroyed his trap and prevented him from trapping animals of the wild. His father advised him to go to Uruk and tell Gilgamesh what had happened. Gilgamesh ordered the hunter-trapper to go to Eanna's temple to seek Shamhat, the harlot, who could seduce Enkidu. The hunter-trapper took Shamhat to the wilderness and let her seduce Enkidu.

SHAMHAT:

A fascinating character who adds to the epic excitement and a lively setting. We can't tell from the story if she is a priestess whose task is to seduce men or a prostitute for hire. Nevertheless, she was successful in seducing Enkidu by showing him her naked body and by making love to him for six days and seven nights. She convinced Enkidu to return with her to Uruk to meet Gilgamesh. She is credited for taming and civilizing Enkidu; without her seduction, Enkidu never would have gone to Uruk and had the chance to meet Gilgamesh.

HUMBABA:

Guardian of the sacred Cedar Forest. He was chosen by Enlil, divine ruler of the earth and winds, to protect the Cedar Forest from intruders. Despite being appointed by the gods to fulfill the duty of protecting the Cedar Forest, Humbaba was depicted in the epic as evil. Disobeying the commands of the gods, Gilgamesh insisted on taking the long journey to the Cedar Forest and killing Humbaba.

Humbaba is powerful and dangerous. He possesses seven shields to protect himself. He can hear, from miles away, all things that move, crawl, or fall. His voice creates a flood, his mouth spits fire, and his breath blows an air of death. Enlil made him a monster to terrify anyone who dared to disturb the sacred Cedar Forest. Fearing the rage of Humbaba, Gilgamesh and Enkidu encouraged each other to enter the Cedar Forest and to defy Humbaba. Humbaba exploded when he heard their footsteps nearing the entrance to the forest. When Humbaba pounded the ground in anger, the earth exploded with a heavy cloud of dust that poured like crushed stones over the heads of Gilgamesh and Enkidu. The two friends staggered to the ground, unaware of what was happening. Then Shamash, the sun god, came to their aid with thirteen blustery winds from all directions that shook Humbaba and set him stumbling to the ground. When Humbaba saw Gilgamesh pointing his ax at him, he went down on his knees and begged Gilgamesh to save his life in return for letting him cut any tree he wants. But Enkidu warned Gilgamesh not to listen to Humbaba's promises and encouraged him to kill Humbaba before Enlil finds out. Humbaba begged Gilgamesh not to listen to Enkidu.

Gilgamesh killed Humbaba and severed his head. They returned to Uruk with Humbaba's head to proclaim it as a trophy for the people of Uruk.

Humbaba was killed fulfilling his duty as a protector of the sacred Cedar Forest—abode of the gods. The gods were angry at Gilgamesh and Enkidu for killing Humbaba; they decided that one of them must die. The killing of Humbaba caused a tragic outcome for Gilgamesh—the loss of his dearest friend, Enkidu.

NINSUN:

Cow goddess, mother of Gilgamesh, wife of Lugalbanda (father of Gilgamesh), Ninsun is a minor priestess. She is known in the epic as wise, quick-witted, and knowledgeable in all matters. She is a caring mother who provides guidance and support to her son, Gilgamesh. When Gilgamesh experiences dreams, he goes to his mother for advice and guidance in interpreting the dreams. Interpreting one of his dreams, Ninsun told her son that someone will touch his life and become his best friend; that someone was Enkidu. Gilgamesh meets Enkidu in Uruk in a lengthy fight, and at the end of the confrontation, they became friends for life. Ninsun adopted Enkidu as a son and appealed to Shamash, the sun god, to protect her son Gilgamesh and his friend Enkidu in their treacherous journey to the Cedar Forest to slain Humbaba. Shamash fulfilled Ninsun's appeal and came to the aid of Gilgamesh when he needed it.

SHAMASH:

The sun god. He is the protector and the personal god for Gilgamesh—helping him during his long and dangerous journey to the Cedar Forest. It was Shamash who helped Gilgamesh and Enkidu defeat Humbaba by blinding him with thirteen blustery winds that set him stumbling to the ground. It was Shamash who disputed the gods' demand to punish Enkidu by telling them that Enkidu was not to blame for the killing of Humbaba.

THE SCORPION MAN AND HIS MATE:

Minor characters who guard the gate at Mount Mashu that leads to the passageway for the sun to set and rise. Their bodies exhibit a furious, half-man, half-scorpion look. When Gilgamesh approached the gate, he ordered the scorpion man to let him pass. The scorpion man took a close look at Gilgamesh and saw in him the face of an exhausted man who came from a long journey. However, he and his mate also detected the look of a divine man in Gilgamesh's makeup. They warned him about the danger he would face if they let him enter the passage way, but Gilgamesh insisted in taking the risk, and they let him in.

SIDURI:

A minor but important character. Her words about life and death, the reality of human existence, and the mystery of immortality add much relevance to the epic. She was an innkeeper by the seashore who helped Gilgamesh find Urshanabi, the ferry-man who led Gilgamesh to

Utanapishtim's dwelling. At first, Siduri was frightened by the exhausted look on Gilgamesh's face and thought that he was a thief and a dangerous man. Fearing his strange look, Siduri locked her doors on Gilgamesh and escaped to the roof. Gilgamesh threatened to break the door if Siduri would not come down and talk to him. When Siduri listened to Gilgamesh talk about the death of his best friend Enkidu and about his fear of death, she felt very sympathetic. She offered Gilgamesh some brilliant advice on the meaning of life and the certainty of death. She also helped him find Urshanabi, Utanapishtim's ferryman, who escorted Gilgamesh to the faraway land where Utanapishtim lives. She warned Gilgamesh about the danger he would encounter in taking the voyage to the dwelling of Utanapishtim.

Siduri, like Ninsun and Shamhat, is a woman who plays an influential role in the epic.

URSHANABI:

Utanapishtim's ferryman. The epic ends with Urshanabi and Gilgamesh admiring the wall of the great city of Uruk as Gilgamesh's greatest achievement.

Gilgamesh met Urshanabi when Siduri showed Gilgamesh the forest where Urshanabi lives. Gilgamesh rushed to the forest and confronted Urshanabi violently. When Urshanabi saw Gilgamesh smashing the magical stones and throwing them into the river, he tried to stop him—but it was too late. Gilgamesh demanded that Urshanabi ferry him to Utanapishtim's dwelling, but Urshanabi told Gilgamesh that without the magical stones, they would not be able to make the journey. "They are the safeguard against the hazardous Waters of Death," regretful Urshanabi told Gilgamesh. Instead, Urshanabi tells Gilgamesh that he must make three hundred paddling poles to get them safely across the Waters of Death. Gilgamesh made all the poles needed to begin their voyage. After a laborious journey crossing the Waters of Death, they finally arrived safely to Utanapishtim's abode.

The absence of the magical stones and the presence of a strange man with Urshanabi aboard the ferry boat made Utanapishtim cautious.

He learned why Gilgamesh wanted to meet him and help him on his quest for eternal life. But Utanapishtim advised Gilgamesh that his quest for immortal life was unattainable. He gave Gilgamesh another chance to prove his willpower and devotion, but Gilgamesh failed the test.

Utanapishtim's wife suggested that Gilgamesh should not go home to Uruk empty-handed. Utanapishtim revealed to him a secret only the gods know—the location of a thorny herbal plant that regenerates youth.

Urshanabi came back to the action again when Utanapishtim was angry at him for bringing Gilgamesh to his shores. Utanapishtim ordered Urshanabi to take Gilgamesh home and not to come back to his shores again. Urshanabi and Gilgamesh left the shores and went to search for the thorny herbal plant. Gilgamesh found the plant and set it aside while he bathed. While Gilgamesh was bathing, a serpent ate the plant. Thus, Gilgamesh returned to Uruk with Urshanabi empty-handed and without any hope in his quest for eternal life.

When they reached the outskirts of Uruk, Gilgamesh showed Urshanabi his monumental wall that will withstand the passage of time. And that is how the epic ended, with Urshanabi and Gilgamesh gazing at the great wall of Uruk in admiration.

UTANAPISHTIM:

Utanapishtim, the faraway, son of King Ubara-Tutu, was a legendary king of Shurupak, a Sumerian city on the bank of the Euphrates River. Everything Gilgamesh was searching for concluded with Utanapishtim telling him the story of his survival from the Great Flood and his ascension by the gods into a perpetual being; everything Gilgamesh was hoping for also concluded there hopelessly.

When Gilgamesh first met Utanapishtim, he thought of him as an ordinary human being, but Gilgamesh realized that Utanapishtim was immortal. When Gilgamesh asked Utanapishtim how he could be granted immortality, Utanapishtim gave him advice about life and death, as Siduri had done. Utanapishtim told Gilgamesh how the gods had a secret meeting where Enlil (god of the earth) decided to destroy humankind, how the gods decided to keep that secret for themselves, and how Ea (god of the of deep water) decided to reveal that secret to him through the walls of the house of reeds.

Utanapishtim revealed the whole story of the Great Flood to Gilgamesh and told him how he built a ship and loaded it with all the living things to escape the flood. After six days and seven nights of downpour and winds and gales, the flood ended, and Utanapishtim and his ship ran aground on Mount Nimush. Utanapishtim offered a sacrifice to the four winds and burned incense on the top of the mountain. When the gods smelled the sweet scent, they gathered around the sacrifice. When Enlil arrived and saw Utanapishtim alive, he became angry at the gods for revealing the secret of obliterating the human race. Utanapishtim told Gilgamesh how Enlil took him by the hand and led him and his wife into the boat, blessed them, and granted them immortality. Utanapishtim told Gilgamesh he might convince the assembly of the gods to look into his quest for immortal life if Gilgamesh could pass a test. He suggested that Gilgamesh stay awake for six days and seven nights, but Gilgamesh failed the test. Then Utanapishtim's wife did not want Gilgamesh to go home empty-handed. She suggested that Utanapishtim should give Gilgamesh another chance. Utanapishtim revealed a secret to Gilgamesh that only the gods know. He showed Gilgamesh the location of a thorny herbal plant that restores youth to old age. Gilgamesh snatched the plant from under the sea and set it aside to bathe. A serpent ate the plant, and Gilgamesh lost all hope in his search for immortality. Accepting the reality of life and death, Gilgamesh returned home with Urshanabi.

Gilgamesh acknowledged Utanapishtim's and Siduri's counsel and became aware of the purpose of his life.

Gods and Goddesses Named in the Epic

ADAD:

The storm god. He bestowed courage and power upon Gilgamesh. In the story, Adad sent the rain to bring destruction to humankind.

THE ANNUNAKI:

Gods of judgment who dictate life and death. They rule the netherworld, where the dead reside. During the flood, they lit their torches and set the land ablaze.

ANTU:

The mother of Ishtar. When Gilgamesh insulted Ishtar and accused her for the suffering she inflicted upon her lovers, Ishtar went to her mother, Antu, and her father, Anu, to beg them to have the Bull of Heaven punish Gilgamesh and to cause havoc and destruction upon the people of Uruk.

ANU:

Father of the gods, god of the sky who resides in seventh heaven. He is also Ishtar's father, who advised her on many subjects, especially when he finally decided to give her the Bull of Heaven. The assembly of the gods gather around Anu when they decide to implement any decision. When the assembly of the gods agreed to send the flood to destroy humanity, they had their secret assembly around their father, Anu. Even the people of Uruk ask for Anu's advice to create a match for Gilgamesh.

ARURU:

Mother goddess, goddess of the creation. She gave Gilgamesh his heavenly body and created Enkidu from a bit of clay.

BELET-SERI:

The scribe of the netherworld who keeps all the deeds of its inhabitants.

EA:

The wisest of the gods. God of the fresh water and the deep sea. He is the god who revealed the secret of the Great Flood to Utanapishtim through the walls of the house of reeds. He advised Utanapishtim to build a ship to escape the flood.

ENLIL:

God of the earth and its inhabitants. He created the Great Flood to destroy every living thing on earth. When Enlil arrived at the gathering around the sacrifice offered by Utanapishtim, he was upset when he found out that Utanapishtim escaped the flood. He wanted to know who revealed the secret, but, in the end, Enlil granted Utanapishtim and his wife eternal life.

ERESHKIGAL:

Ruler of the netherworld. In a dream, Enkidu heard Ereshkigal questioning Belet-seri, the scribe of the netherworld, about how Enkidu ended up in the netherworld. This dream frightened Enkidu and made him believe that his end was near.

THE IGIGI:

They are assigned to the great god of heaven and the netherworld. At the gathering of the gods of heaven around Utanapishtim's sacrifice, Enlil questioned the Igigi about how Utanapishtim escaped the destruction of the Great Flood.

MAMITUM:

Goddess of destiny who dictates the time of life and the time of death for humankind. The fate of humankind is kept a secret—only the gods know.

NIRGAL:

God of the plague and war who opened the barriers of the undercurrent to let the water flood the land and sweep away every living thing.

NINURTA:

God of agriculture, son of Enlil, who opened the protective dam and made the deep water pouring all over the land to create the Great Flood. He is also the symbol of vitality.

NISABA:

God of the grain. Enkidu cherished some of Nisaba's traits.

SHILLAT AND HANISH:

Messengers of the storms. In the epic, Adad, god of the thunderstorm, steered the clouds to create thunderous rain to flood the land. Shillat and Hanish went ahead of Adad, gliding over the land to make way for the storms to pass through the hills and the mountains.

SIN:

The moon god. Gilgamesh appealed to Sin and other gods to help Enkidu as he rested in the netherworld. During his long journey after the death of Enkidu, Gilgamesh rested near a mountain pass where he spent the night frightened by the roaring of lions. Gilgamesh looked at the moon and begged Sin to give him the courage to kill the lions and continue his long journey without fear and without facing any danger.

About the Translations

Writing was invented in Iraq over five thousand years ago, and everything said before that time is gone forever. Some scholars believe that *The Epic of Gilgamesh* was first delivered orally, but other scholars disagree with that theory. They believe that the epic was first written in Sumerian. Whatever the case, the epic passed through stages of development and was rewritten and edited by many generations.

The early *Epic of Gilgamesh* was first written in Sumerian—a language with unknown origin and not related to any other known language. The tablets that we refer to as the standard version comprise the longest and most complete version. The tablets were discovered in the ruins of the library of King Ashurbanipal in Nineveh by Henry Layard and Hurmuzd Rassam and later by George Smith. The story was written in standard Babylonian, a dialect of Akkadian practiced by scribes who used this dialect for writing mostly literary work. As mentioned earlier in this introduction, the standard version was edited and rewritten in the middle Babylonian period between 1400 BC and 1000 BC by Sin-leqi-unninni. By using his poetic skill, Sin-leqi-unninni edited his version of the epic from the old Babylonian period (2000–1500 BC).

During the thousand years or so between the epic's inception and Sin-leqi-unninni's version, the language might have changed. To illustrate how language changes, I picked up a line from Shakespeare's *Romeo and Juliet*, where the nurse responds to Juliet's question in act 2:

> O God's lady dear,
> Are you so hot? Mary, come up, I trow.

I couldn't find the word *trow* in any dictionary. Even automatic correction on my computer warns me with a red underline. I found out that "God's lady" meant the Virgin Mary, and "Mary, come up, I trow" is an expression of irritation during Shakespeare's time. Many people of our time find it difficult to read Shakespeare's language because of vast changes in language and lifestyle over the past four hundred years. We can imagine, then, how language changed during the last five thousand years. Thus, I hold in high esteem all the archeologists who have been involved in transliteration and translation of a language that is so old and so difficult to delve into its past and to find some idioms that are closely related to the original.

The procedure of transliteration is an intricate one. It involves deciphering the alphabets from cuneiform letters and its phonetic morphemes into other alphabets. It takes an effort to determine the correct letter or vowel that corresponds to the source text. Some versions of the same source text could be different than another version, in which case a decision is made about what corresponds closely to the original. Sometimes it is a guess, but the result has to be agreed upon among scholars. And this will take them into another step—translation.

Translation is the process of interpreting the meaning of the text that is already formatted in coded letters from the original deciphered cuneiform inscription. Translators, relying on their knowledge of cuneiform, can relay the closest message in their own language. Translators also take into account constraints that include context, the rules of grammar of the two languages, writing conventions, and idioms. Sometimes translators guess at the meaning of the words that have no match for this language—idioms can especially be problematic. The deciphered manuscript can have different meanings by different translators, as we see in *The Epic of Gilgamesh*. Furthermore, the translated manuscript can take another step through literary translation that gives the meaning more acceptance to readers.

Many modern writers and poets have modified some deciphered manuscripts into a contemporary language. Despite their unfamiliarity with cuneiform, some have succeeded in reproducing a fair and a fine literary work. As for myself, I have tried to translate the existing work of many scholars into my own literal translation.

My Adaptation of The Epic of Gilgamesh

First, I have to give credit to all of the scholars who dedicated their life to deciphering and translating the epic from its original tablets. They let us enjoy the beauty of the oldest literary work in the history of humankind that was hidden for more than four thousand years.

The translations of many scholars benefited me tremendously in putting together my own adaptation of the epic. I have conducted an elaborate study of eight well-known scholars who have done a great work in translating the epic, and I also have benefited from the Arabic translation by two well-known Middle Eastern scholars. I also gathered all I could from other writers who had re-created the epic with their own version. After I assimilated all the work, I came up with my own conclusion, which is a little different from other works, but I kept the original theme as comprehensible as I could.

My adaptation of the epic is not meant to be a reference for scholars, but they are welcome to assess it. I used the standard version that was edited and rewritten from the old Babylonian version by Sin-leqi-unninni. I also filled in some gaps and missing words in some of the original translations with my own words. I clarified and substituted some archaic words that are troubling to readers of modern poetry. I also reworked some lines into a simplified free verse.

When appropriate, I used dialogue in my composition. I use a style of free verse that doesn't follow a regular pattern or a steady backbeat. I use both short lines and long lines in my composition—Frank O'Hara and Allen Ginsburg both combine short and long lines with harmony. I also use initial repetition (anaphora) as Walt Whitman did in (*Leaves of Grass*). Regardless of what I have altered or what liberties I have taken in my composition, I coherently retained the thematic basis of the epic.

Finally, I acknowledge the scholars and others who made their work helpful: Andrew George with his outstanding new translation of the epic; Herbert Mason with his verse narrative of the epic; Maureen Gallery Kovacs, Benjamin Foster, and Nancy Sanders with her 1972 literary translation of the epic; John Gardner and John Maier for their fine translation and rendering of the epic;, Yanita Chen; and, last but not least, the late Taha Baqir and his Arabic translation of the epic from its original cuneiform.

Notes

Diverging from conventional practice, I have not used footnotes in my introduction, because I feel they can distract the reader and interrupt the flow of information. Supplementing my information are sources listed in the following bibliography.

Bibliography

Alsawah, Firas. *Gilgamesh.* Dar Ala'a Aldin, Damascus, 1996.

Baqir, Taha. *Mulhamet Gilgamesh, Odeesut Al-Iraq Al-khalideh.* Iraq Ministry of Information Publication, 1975.

Cottrel, Leronard. *The Quest for Sumer.* New York: G. P. Putnam's Sons, 1965.

Dalley, Stephanie. *Myth from Mesopotamia: Creation, the Flood, Gilgamesh, and others.* Oxford, England: Oxford University Press, 2000.

Ferry, David. *Gilgamesh: A New Rendering in English Verse.* New York: Farrar, Straus and Giroux, 1993.

Fiore, Silvestro. *Voices from the Clay: The Development of Assyro-Babylonian Literature.* Norman: University of Oklahoma Press, 1965.

Foster, Benjamin. *The Epic of Gilgamesh.* New York: W. W. Norton, 2001.

Gardner, John, and John Maier. *Gilgamesh: The Version of Sin-leqi-unninni.* New York: Alfred A. Knopf, 1984.

George, Andrew R. *The Epic of Gilgamesh: A New translation.* New York: Barnes and Noble, 1999.

George, Andrew R. *The Babylonian Gilgamesh Epic: Introduction, Critical Edition and Cuneiform Text.* 2 Vols. Oxford, England: Oxford University Press, 2003.

Gordon, Cyrus H. *Forgotten Scripts: Their Ongoing Discovery and Decipherment.* New York: Dorset Press, 1987.

Jacobsen, Thorkild. *The Sumerian King List.* Chicago: University of Chicago Press, 1993.

Heidel, Alexander. *The Gilgamesh Epic and Old Testament Parallels.* Chicago: University of Chicago Press, 1949.

Kovacs, Maureen Gallery. *The Epic of Gilgamesh.* Stanford, CA: Stanford University Press, 1989.

Kramer, S. N. *History Begins at Sumer.* London: Thames & Hudson, 1958.

Mason, Herbert. *Gilgamesh: A Verse Narrative*. Boston: Houghton Mifflin, 1971.

Olson, Steve. *Mapping Human History: Genes, Race, and Our Common Origin*. Boston: Mariner Books, 2003.

Sanders, Nancy K. *The Epic of Gilgamesh*. Harmondsworth: Penguin, 1972.

Stewart, Rory. *The Prince of the Marshes*. Orlando, FL: Harcourt, 2006.

Temple, Robert. *He Who Saw Everything. A Verse Version of the Epic of Gilgamesh*. London: Rider, 1991.

Tigay, Jeffrey H. *The Evolution of the Gilgamesh Epic*. Philadelphia: University of Pennsylvania Press, 1982.

"This is a story that exhibits a striking meaning of life and death, of love and friendship, and of one's deeds.

This is the oldest literary composition in the history of human civilization; its theme has a wide scope that is relevant to modern life.

This is the story of Gilgamesh, king of Uruk—the greatest city of its time. Is it a mythical or historical tale? It may be conceived as either or both."

— Sam Kuraishi

The Epic
of
Gilgamesh

A NEW ADAPTATION

by Sam Kuraishi

Inscription I
PROLOGUE

He who felt the deep meaning of life;
he who reached the faraway land in search of the mystery
of his own existence, and came back to his beloved city
of Uruk with courage, virtue, and wisdom.

He who walked the most treacherous roads
to the Cedar Forest, killed its guardian
rancorous Humbaba—the most dangerous
creature of his time—and cut the biggest tree in the forest
to erect a monumental door for Eanna's temple.

He who challenged the wilderness, killed lions and beasts,
dug wells in the arid lands, cut passages to the mountains,
crossed the Waters of Death,
and dived into the bed of the deepest sea.
He who built the greatest wall
his world has ever known.

He is Gilgamesh, king of the great city of Uruk.
Supreme among kings;
nothing like him ever was!

What is his glory?
Isn't the magnificent wall of the great city of Uruk
his everlasting monument?

Did the Seven Sages not style its structure?

The great city of Uruk, the glory of the world;
nothing like it ever was!
Look at its fire-hardened brick wall,
examine its splendor, and observe its structure—fire-
hardened bricks laid by the hands of the Seven Sages.
Every brick sparkles like bright copper.
Nothing like it ever was!

Step on the threshold and enter the gate,
climb the stairways and walk on top of the wall,
look below and see Uruk's brilliant plan:
three and a half miles its expanse,
one square mile its city dwellings,
one square mile its date palms and fruit grove,
one square mile its meadows.
Nothing like it ever was!

Step down and enter Eanna's temple,
move inside its one-half mile stretch
and marvel its stunning structure.
Nothing like it ever was!

Go into the foundation and search for the copper box,
unfasten its lock and open its lid,
read the inscriptions on the lapis lazuli, and find
how Gilgamesh challenged everything in his lifelong
search for the unknown and came back rational and wise.

Gilgamesh
Wild bull Gilgamesh, son of divine king Lugalbanda,
offspring of cow goddess Ninsun, by virtue of whom
he was two-thirds divine, one-third human—a godlike man
of unmatched power.
Heavenly body shaped by Aruru, goddess of the creation,

striking appeal blessed by Shamash, the sun god,
remarkable strength linked to Adad, the storm god.

Gilgamesh, fierce and brave.
He can demolish a stone wall
with his powerful arms.

He rages like a roaring lion,
he charges like a raging bull,
he marches in front, trusted as a leader,
he marches in the back, trusted as a protector,
he is strong in his afflictions—head always up.

Who built the great wall of the great city of Uruk?
Who dug wells and cleared passages to the mountains?
Who dived into the deepest water and sailed into the Sea
of Death?
It is Gilgamesh, the daring king.

Gilgamesh, protector of his city,
feared and loved by his people,
and when he discharges his weapons,
he is trusted by all and feared by all.

He drafts young men at his own will,
he lets no son see his father,
he lets no daughter see her mother,
he claims sexual rights over young women,
he lets no virgin sleep with her bridegroom;
on the beats of the drums,
he wakes his subjects at will.

Citizen's Complaint
Daughters of the warriors, young brides, fathers, and sons
complained to the gods to listen to their frustrations.

The citizens of Uruk speak to the gods:
> You created wild bull Gilgamesh; no one can
> challenge his power.
> Fierce and savage, tyrant and oppressor, he drafts
> all the young men and claims sexual rights
> over young women.
> We appeal to you, gods, to create a match
> to challenge Gilgamesh.

∾

Anu, father of the gods, lord of the sky, heard their
complaint and called upon mother goddess Aruru,
creator of humankind, goddess of birth, to create
a match to defy Gilgamesh.

Anu speaks to Aruru:
> You created Gilgamesh with unmatched strength,
> smart and wise, fierce and savage, tyrant but beloved.
> I appeal to you to create a man
> who can rival Gilgamesh,
> a man who can challenge Gilgamesh
> and let the citizens of Uruk live in peace.

∾

The creation of Enkidu
Aruru wetted her hands, kneaded a lump of clay
and cast it into the wilderness.
Aruru created wild Enkidu from clay—no inception.
He made the wilderness his habitat,
he lived and roamed with the creatures of the wild,
and knew nothing outside his wilderness.
Enkidu, his shaggy hair extends way below his shoulders;
it ripples like wild grass on a windy day—a trait of
Nisaba, god of the grain.

His body hair covers him like a garb—a trait of
Sumugan, god of the cattle.
His strong muscles thrust like a violent wind—a makeup of
Ninurta, god of the thunderstorm.

Enkidu, friend of the wilderness,
protector of the wild animals,
eats with them, drinks with them,
sleeps with them, and protects them
from hunters and trappers.

A trapper spotted Enkidu near a watering hole drinking water
and eating grass with his wild friends.
The trapper was horrified by the strange look
of this wild man.
He panicked and fled to tell his father what he had seen.

The trapper speaks to his father:
    My father, I saw a strange-looking man,
    he roams the wilderness with animals of the wild,
    he is big and muscular and wears no clothes,
    he is as powerful as a fallen meteor,
    he is as hairy as a wild cow, as strong as a wild bull,
    he drinks water and eats grass with the wild animals,
    he protects them from hunters and trappers,
    he capped my pit, destroyed my traps,
    and let the animals escape.
    I was afraid to be near him or to stop him.

The trapper's father speaks to his son:
    My son, the answer dwells in Uruk,
    where Gilgamesh is the mighty king.
    Take the road to Uruk, my son, and tell Gilgamesh
    what you have witnessed; Gilgamesh will listen to
    your grievance. He will send Shamhat, the prostitute
    who masters the art of seduction.

When you spot this wild man near the water hole
eating and drinking with the animals of the wild,
let Shamhat's heavenly body lure him,
let her strip naked and expose her heaving breast,
let her lie on her back and spread her legs.
And when his animal friends see him feeling
her naked body, they will mistrust him and reject him.

∽

Listening to his father's advice, the trapper headed
to Uruk to tell King Gilgamesh
about the wild man he saw.

The trapper speaks to Gilgamesh:
    King Gilgamesh, I saw a terrifying wild man
    who lives in the wilderness with wild animals,
    he is as strong as a fallen meteor,
    he is as hairy as a cow, as strong as a wild bull,
    he drinks and grazes with wild animals,
    he protects them from hunters and trappers,
    he capped my pits, destroyed my traps
    and let the animals escape.
    I was afraid to stop him.

∽

Gilgamesh speaks to the trapper:
    Go now to Eanna's temple and seek
    Shamhat the prostitute; she possesses
    a magical power of seducing men.

    Take Shamhat with you to the wilderness
    where the wild man roams,
    wait until you see him near the watering hole
    with the animals of wild,

let Shamhat use her heavenly body to entice him,
let her strip naked and expose her heaving breast,
let her lie on her back and spread her legs,
and when he sees her, he will embrace her.
After the animals see him embracing her naked body,
they will mistrust him and reject him.

Civilizing Enkidu
The trapper went to Eanna's temple;
took Shamhat with him and accompanied her
to the wilderness.

On the third day of their journey, they reached the site
and sat there and waited for two days.
And on the third day, Enkidu and the wild animals came
near the watering hole to drink and eat.

Enkidu, joined his wild friends at the watering hole,
drank water with them,
ate grass and herbage with them,
and shared all his pleasure with them.

The trapper speaks to Shamhat:
Hurry Shamhat and get ready,
practice your art of seduction,
take off your clothes and lay on your back,
show him your breast and your naked body,
show him your channel and spread your legs,
let him squeeze you and board you;
when his animal friends catch sight of him,
they will walk out on him and abandon him.

Shamhat put her talent to work: exposed her naked
body and waited for Enkidu to explore her exhibition!

Enkidu caught sight of her and drew close to her.
He gazed in wonder and surprise at her naked body.
Then rested his hairy body upon her soft naked body
and entered her.

During the duration of making love, Enkidu's genitalia
stayed erect for six days and seven nights; he never
had such a pleasure like this with his animal friends!

His first sexual intercourse with a woman satisfied
his frame of mind for a while, he grew a little weary
from the lengthy sexual intercourse,
and decided to go back and join his animal friends,
but they rejected him and turned away from him.

He tried to run and join them, but he failed;
his knees were weak, his strength was drained,
and his body was exhausted from
the prolonged copulation.

Realizing what had happened, Enkidu returned
to Shamhat and rested by her feet.
He looked at her with admiration,
she looked at him with anticipation,
and a period of silence befell upon them.

Shamhat speaks to Enkidu:
> Enkidu, you are delightful to look at,
> you are blessed with physical attraction and strength.
> Why are you roaming the hills and the meadows
> with the wild beasts?
> Why are you dwelling in a no-man's-land?

Come with me to the great city of Uruk,
let me lead you into the world of civilization,
and let me show you how Gilgamesh
rules the great city of Uruk with his blatant
and undisputed power that none of his subjects
can challenge.

~

Enkidu speaks to Shamhat:
Take me to Uruk, where Gilgamesh rules
his subjects unchallenged.
I will face him in defiance;
I will show him who is the strongest and the mightiest!

I, Enkidu, who is raised with the beasts,
who has no equal, is the strongest and the mightiest.

Shamhat speaks to Enkidu:
Enkidu, come with me to the great city of Uruk
where lively women dress in tempting style,
where cheerful men dress in appealing fashion,
where charming harlots parade in the street corners
with their alluring bodies,
where days and nights are bursting with festivals,
where the young and the old dance
on the beat of the drums.

Enkidu, come with me and I will show you
the pleasure of life!
Come with me and I will show you mighty Gilgamesh,
the steadfast, the powerful,
who is awake and alert day and night.

Shamash, the sun god, his protector,
blessed him with love,

the gods, Anu, Enlil, and Ea conferred him
with power and wisdom.
Gilgamesh is stronger and taller than you.
Whatever he desires, no one can stand in his way.

Gilgamesh had many dreams about a man like you;
his mother told him that a man like you is the focus
of his dreams.
In his first dream, Gilgamesh revealed to his mother
that he saw a star of heaven shooting forth light;
one star fell by him like a meteorite.
He wanted to lift it, but it was too heavy,
he wanted to move it, but he couldn't.
People of Uruk gathered around it,
the crowd cuddled it and kissed it like it was
a newly born child.
He looked at it and loved it,
he embraced it and kissed it like it was
a wife to him.
He moved it and placed it at his mother's feet;
she treated it like a son to her.

And his mother, cow goddess Ninsun, the wise,
the quick-witted, who is knowledgeable in all matters,
interpreted his first dream.

She comforted her son and let him realize that
the star he embraced and kissed like a wife,
the star that he placed at her feet,
was a man who will be his friend and protector,
a man who will come to him
from the wilderness blessed with
the courage of god of the sky Anu.

She told her son that the man he will meet
is as strong as a rock;

as powerful as a meteorite.
And when he will look at him,
he will embrace him and love him
like a man embracing his wife.

Mother Ninsun reassured her son that the man
he will meet will be a trustworthy friend,
will stand by his side, and will never abandon him.

Gilgamesh went on to tell his mother about
a second dream he experienced.

He told his mother that he saw people
in a public square of Uruk gazing at an ax;
they were amazed by its size.
And when he saw the ax, he embraced it like a man
embracing his wife,
he moved it and placed it at his mother's feet,
and his mother dealt with it like a son to her.

And his mother, cow goddess Ninsun, the wise,
the quick-witted, who is knowledgeable in all matters,
interpreted his second dream with good omen.
She told her son that the ax he saw in his dream,
where he placed it at her feet, was a man
who will be his lifelong friend and a brother forever.
She assured her son that he will embrace and love
this strange man like a man loves his wife.

Considering the blissful clarification of
his two dreams, Gilgamesh appealed to his mother
and to Enlil, god of the earth and it inhabitants,
to bless him with a man who can trust;
a man who can share his life with.

Inscription II
TAMING ENKIDU

After telling the dreams to Enkidu,
Shamhat exposed her soft legs and let Enkidu lay
between them.
Enkidu embraced Shamhat and began to make love to her for six days
and seven nights.
Coupling with Shamhat and making repeated love to her,
Enkidu abandoned his desire to go back
to the wilderness to join his animal friends.

Shamhat speaks to Enkidu:
    Enkidu, you are a godlike,
    you are strong and attractive.
    Why don't you leave the wild life and come with me
    to Uruk, where you can meet Gilgamesh.
    Gilgamesh is big, brave, and powerful, and no one
    could match his might.
    You will love him and embrace him like a man
    embracing his wife.

                ∽

Shamhat looked at Enkidu's face and sensed his feeling.
She took off her clothes and tore it into two pieces,
she dressed his naked body with one piece
and wrapped herself with the other.

They held hands and left the wilderness behind.

The Taming of Enkidu
After a long journey, they reached a shepherd's village.
The shepherds gathered around Enkidu in admiration.

The shepherds speak among themselves:
> This man is an extraordinary man.
> He is tall, strong, and fearless—a match for Gilgamesh.
> He who is raised with the animals of the wild,
> gazed with them and drank their milk,
> is as powerful as them.

❧

Enkidu never sat at a dining table
or ate bread and drank wine.
He was raised with wild animals, ate and drank
with them, and drew milk from them.
The shepherds sat Enkidu beside Shamhat at
the dining table, where Shamhat gave him
a loaf of bread and a jug of wine.

Shamhat speaks to Enkidu:
> Eat your bread, Enkidu,
> drink your wine,
> have a feast,
> drink to life,
> and savor the pleasure of the moment.

❧

Enkidu, for the first time in his life, ate the bread
and drank seven fillings of wine.
His face flickered,
he felt the pleasure of eating and drinking,

and began dancing and singing to life.

The shepherds trimmed Enkidu's long hair,
shaved his hairy body, massaged him
with scented oil, dressed him with fine clothing,
and armed him with weapons.
He became a civilized man; a hunter and a warrior.
He fought lions and chased wolves and became
the village watchman.
Earning his trust, the shepherds slept the nights
comfortably and free of fear.

While making love to Shamhat, Enkidu spotted a man
walking by with a load on his back.
Enkidu was uneasy when he saw the man rushing
hurriedly with the heavy load.
He wanted to question him.

Enkidu speaks to Shamhat:
> Bring that man to me, Shamhat.
> I want to know why he is rushing
> and where he is going with a heavy load on his back.
> This man looks exhausted and agitated.

Shamhat, by Enkidu's demand, stopped the man
and requested that he accompany her to meet Enkidu.

The man speaks to Enkidu:
> In the great city of Uruk, where Gilgamesh is king,
> the people are celebrating a wedding festival
> for the young; I have to be there to set tables
> and to prepare food.
> Gilgamesh will lead a parade,
> he will choose a virgin bride to sleep with

before the bridegroom does.
It is destined, and by the order of the gods,
that Gilgamesh sleeps with the bride before
the newlywed does.

ᕦᕤ

Enkidu flew into a rage when he heard the passerby
telling him how Gilgamesh treats a bride-to-be.
He told Shamhat to take him to Uruk;
so he can stop Gilgamesh from exercising his right.

The Confrontation
Shamhat took Enkidu to Uruk.
They walked the road as fast as they could.
As Enkidu entered the gate of the great city of Uruk,
people in the streets followed him,
surrounded him and praised him,
and admired his physique.

People of Uruk speak of Enkidu:
This man is mighty strong,
this man is a match for Gilgamesh.
He is shorter in height,
but equal in size.

He was raised with the animals of the wild
and earned their trust,
he drank their milk and acquired their strength,
and he is as powerful and as energetic as his
animal friends.

ᕦᕤ

On the beat of the drums, the procession marched
to the house of the virgin to be taken—Gilgamesh

in the lead.
Gilgamesh reached the house where the bride
was lying in her bed.
Enkidu blocked the door and stopped Gilgamesh
from entering; they bumped each other
like raging bulls; the fight began.

They fought all night, grappling and wrestling,
crushing doors and cracking walls,
shaking pillars and braking windows.
With his powerful hands, Gilgamesh clutched Enkidu
and tossed him to the ground.
Gilgamesh held Enkidu's hand
and helped him to stand on his feet.
And when the fight was over,
they looked at each other, hugged each other, and laughed.

Enkidu speaks to Gilgamesh:
    Wild bull Gilgamesh, brave and fearless,
    you are majestic among kings.
    Your mother, wild cow Ninsun, blessed you
    with courage and pride,
    Enlil wanted you to raise your head high,
    and gave you the privilege to be a great king.

∽

The hostility stopped and the friendship began.
The two acknowledged each other as equal.
They hugged each other and kissed each other
as if nothing had happened.
And that was the birth of an everlasting friendship.

The Friendship
Gilgamesh decided to take a long and a risky journey to
the Cedar Forest to kill rancorous Humbaba and to cut

the tallest cedar tree to make a monumental door
for Eanna's temple.
He wanted Enkidu to accompany him on his long journey,
but Enkidu warned Gilgamesh of the risk he was taking
if he tried to challenge Humbaba.

Enkidu speaks to Gilgamesh:
> My dear Gilgamesh, abandon this long and risky
> journey to the Cedar Forest.
> I have explored this terrain, it is unsafe,
> the roads are dangerous,
> Humbaba is excessively vicious,
> and killing him would be a very challenging task.

ᢙ

Ninsun, concerned about the long journey
her son Gilgamesh insisted to take,
appealed to Shamash, the sun god, to protect
her son on his hazardous journey.

Ninsun speaks to Shamash:
> Sun god Shamash, I am raising my hands;
> appealing to you to protect my son and his friend
> against Humbaba's aggression.
> I am appealing to you to bring my son and his friend
> back to Uruk out of harm's way.

ᢙ

Ninsun speaks to her son, Gilgamesh:
> My beloved son, be kind to your friend Enkidu,
> he has no one to lean on but you,
> he will stand by you,
> he will sacrifice his life for you.

ᢙ

68

Enkidu couldn't suppress his feeling when he heard
the caring words Ninsun told her son Gilgamesh
about him.
He was overwhelmed by Ninsun's words,
he could not hide his deep emotion,
his cheeks were flooded with tears,
his whole body was quivering,
and his legs couldn't hold his weight.

Enkidu speaks to Gilgamesh:
    My friend, why do you want to take this long
    and dangerous journey?
    The Cedar Forest is too far to reach,
    it is a mammoth forest with miles of dense plants,
    and I know how hazardous that terrain is.

    Humbaba is a very strong and dangerous creature,
    he can hear things that move, crawl, or fall
    from miles away,
    his voice is louder than a thunder,
    and his breath is more destructive than a flash of fire.

    Enlil placed him there to protect the sacred forest,
    no one dares to trespass its boundaries,
    and if anyone tries,
    he is destined to die.

                        ✣

Gilgamesh speaks to Enkidu:
    Why does fear fret you, my friend?
    You were raised in the wilderness,
    and stood courageous in the face of danger.
    Lions feared you, animals of the forest feared you,
    and hunters and trappers feared you.

My friend Enkidu, I shall defy danger,
and shall travel to the end of the world
to confront Humbaba and kill him.

If Humbaba kills me, my people will say that
Gilgamesh died as a martyr,
and if I kill him, my people will say that
Gilgamesh lives as a hero.

I shall never surrender to fear,
I shall prove to the world that I can kill this monster
and enter the Cedar Forest and cut any tree I want.
My friend Enkidu, let us prepare for the long journey
to the Cedar Forest,
let us head to the forge and have our skilled craftsmen
cast the best metals to make the finest weapons
ever made.

Gilgamesh held Enkidu's hand and headed for the forge.
He ordered the blacksmiths to make the weapons they needed for the
journey: hatchets, each weighing 198 pounds,
swords, each weighing 132 pounds,
gold latches, each weighing 33 pounds.

Gilgamesh and Enkidu left the forge; each carried
a heavy load of 600 pounds of newly forged weapons.
They marched to the city plaza, where the council of the
elders, young warriors, men and women, young and old,
cheered them and blessed them on their lengthy journey.

Gilgamesh speaks to the citizens of Uruk:
    My beloved citizens of the great city of Uruk,
    council of the elders, young warriors, men and women,
    young and old, I have determined to take

the long journey to the Cedar Forest
and to challenge rancorous Humbaba.

I want to let the world know
who is the mightiest man of his time.
If I die, do not feel sorry for me,
for sorrow is for the weak.
And with the blessing of my protector Shamash,
I shall come back to you victorious.
You too shall bless me and encourage me
to invade the Cedar Forest and defy
its guardian, rancorous Humbaba.

And when I return to you with Humbaba's head
and the tallest tree from the Cedar Forest,
I will build a monumental door
for Eanna's temple,
I will celebrate with you
the new year festival twice,
I will sing with you and dance with you
on the beats of the drums
and the sounds of the horns.

Enkidu speaks to the council of the elders:
    I appeal to you, council of the elders,
    to stop Gilgamesh from going to the Cedar Forest.
    I know the road well; it is dangerous
    and unpredictable.
    I know Humbaba well; he is monstrous and frightful.
    His voice is louder than thunder,
    his breath is more destructive than a flash of fire,
    and his ear can hear any sound from miles away.

Enlil placed him there to protect the sacred forest,
and if anyone who dares to enter the forest
and challenge him,
death will descend upon him.

∽

The council of the elders speaks to Gilgamesh:
Our beloved king, we know you are young and strong.
Do not depend on your strength alone,
do not let your feeling and your courage
overcome reasoning.
Enkidu knows Humbaba well, and he knows
how vicious and dangerous he is.
Enlil put him there to protect the sacred Cedar Forest,
and anyone who dares to enter the forest
will face danger and death.

∽

Gilgamesh listened to the advice of the council
of the elders, shook his head in disapproval,
and looked at Enkidu to get his reaction.

Gilgamesh speaks to Enkidu:
My brother, my friend, no one can discourage
me from going to the Cedar Forest
and killing rancorous Humbaba.

I don't want to sit on my throne idle.
I am determined to take this long journey
to beat the unbeatable.

∽

Inscription III
PREPARING FOR THE JOURNEY

After listening to the advice of Enkidu and the council
of the elders, Gilgamesh insisted upon taking the long
journey to the Cedar Forest to defeat Humbaba.

The council of the elders speaks to Gilgamesh:
>   Be careful on your long journey,
>   don't rely on yourself only, let Enkidu be by your side.
>   Enkidu is a trustworthy friend,
>   he knows the terrain well,
>   he can guide you and protect you.
>   He is tried in combat, he fought lions and beasts
>   in the plains and the mountains.
>   And with Shamash safeguard,
>   we are confident to see you and Enkidu come back
>   to our beloved Uruk victorious.

Gilgamesh and Enkidu went to Ninsun, the wise,
the quick-witted, to seek her guidance.
At the sanctum, Gilgamesh knelt before his mother
Ninsun and asked for her blessing.

Gilgamesh speaks to his mother, Ninsun:
>   Bless me, my mother, on my long journey
>   to the Cedar Forest, and pray for me to come to you

safe and victorious.
Appeal to Shamash to protect me on my long journey,
beg him to grant me the strength to defeat Humbaba.

Dear mother, I want you to greet me at the gate
upon my safe return, and let the people of Uruk
celebrate my homecoming in a great style.

∽

Ninsun left for her private confine, took off her clothes,
wrapped up a bunch of tamarisk, soaked it in fresh
water and soapwort, and used it to purified her body.
She dressed in a ceremonial outfit,
put on a precious necklace, decorated her head
with her royal crown, and went to the roof
to burn a sweet-smelling incense.

She raised her hands, faced the sun,
and appealed to sun god Shamash.

Ninsun speaks to Shamash:
Sun god Shamash, you granted my son a demanding
heart and an obsessive mind.
He is obsessed with his plan to take the long
and hazardous journey to a land unknown to him.

I ask you, sun god, to strengthen his arms and
legs, to bless him with courage,
to safeguard him with more daylight than eventide,
and to lend him your supernatural power to defeat
rancorous Humbaba.

Sun god Shamash, as you deliver the end of the day
to your father Sin, the moon god,
 when the moon grows bright
over the creatures of the night,

let Aya, your brave wife, goddess of dawn,
remind you to watch over my son
and his friend Enkidu during the night.

༄

After appealing to Shamash, Ninsun extinguished
the burning incense, went down to her private
confine, and told Enkidu to stand by her side.

Ninsun speaks to Enkidu:
    My dear Enkidu, my womb did not bear you,
    but I have chosen you as a brother to my son.
    I am placing this precious locket around your neck,
    and letting the ritual women, the servants,
    and the priestesses be my witness as I embrace you
    to be my son and a brother to my son Gilgamesh.

    I want you to show my son a safe passage
    to the Cedar Forest.
    You have roamed the wilderness,
    you are familiar with the treacherous terrain,
    and you know how dangerous Humbaba is.

    May Shamash help you with his magical force
    to defeat rancorous Humbaba,
    may he shelter you on your lengthy
    and hazardous journey,
    may he bring you back to our beloved Uruk
    safe and victorious.

Gilgamesh and Enkidu embraced each other, held hands,
and went to the council of the elders
to bid them farewell and to advise them on running Uruk
during their absence.

Gilgamesh speaks to the council of the elders:
    Until we kill Humbaba and show the world
    who is stronger,
    until we bring his head with the most precious
    cedar tree ever was,
    you must help the young and the old,
    you must oversee justice to the people of Uruk,
    you must share in the protection of your beloved city.

                                 ᢙ

People of Uruk marched behind their king
wishing him a safe return.
Young and old saluted their king
and chanted: "long live our king."

The council of the elders speaks to Gilgamesh:
    Rely on Enkidu and seek his advice.
    He is a trustworthy friend,
    he knows the rough courses and the passageways
    that lead to the Cedar Forest,
    and he knows how vicious Humbaba is.
    He tried in battles; he is a courageous man.

    May Shamash help you with his magical force
    to defeat rancorous Humbaba and come back
    to our great city of Uruk unharmed and victorious.

                                 ᢙ

The council of the elders speaks to Enkidu:
    We want you, our dear friend Enkidu, to give
    Gilgamesh the support when he is distressed,
    to lead him to the roads you are familiar with,
    and to warn him about the danger he might encounter
    at the Cedar Forest where Humbaba dwells.

You were born in the wilderness and lived among
animals of the wild,
and you know how to survive
in the most dangerous terrain.
As you travel the dangerous roads,
we want you to share your experience with Gilgamesh,
and to lead him to the right path on your journey
 to the Cedar Forest safe.

Inscription IV

THE JOURNEY TO THE CEDAR FOREST

After traveling one hundred and thirty-five miles,
they rested, fed themselves well, and resumed their trip.
After traveling one hundred and ninety-six miles,
they camped for the night; at the end of one day
they traveled three hundred and thirty-five miles.
In three days they traveled a close distance
of one thousand miles from Uruk to the outskirts
of Mount Lebanon—a ninety-day journey
for normal travelers.
At sunset, they dug a well near a mountain and filled
their water skins with fresh water.
Gilgamesh climbed the mountain, spread a sacred flour,
uplifted his head to heaven, faced the sun, and appealed
to Shamash to bestow upon him a pleasant dream.
At nighttime, Enkidu set up a tent to protect Gilgamesh
from the cold night wind, rested him on the ground,
encircled him with a sacred flour and hoped
that Gilgamesh could have a wishful dream.
With his chin resting on his knees, Gilgamesh went into
a normal sleep, but woke up confused.

Gilgamesh speaks to Enkidu:
    My friend Enkidu, I feel pain in my whole body,
    I feel stiffness in my arms and legs.

Did you touch me and awaken me?
Did a god pass by me?
My friend, I had a terrifying dream,
and I am dreadfully confused.
I saw a mountain falling on me; its massive weight
made me feel like a tiny creature crushed under
a huge rock.

⌒

Enkidu speaks to Gilgamesh:
My friend, the dream you had is a gesture of hope;
the mountain was Humbaba.
With the help of your protector Shamash, the sun god,
we shall destroy Humbaba and eradicate
his name from this world.

⌒

After traveling one hundred and thirty-five miles,
they rested, fed themselves well, and resumed their trip.
After traveling one hundred and ninety-six miles,
they camped for the night; at the end of one day
they traveled three hundred and thirty-five miles.
In three days they traveled a close distance
of one thousand miles from Uruk to the outskirts
of Mount Lebanon—a ninety-day journey
for a normal traveler.

At nighttime, Enkidu put up a tent to protect Gilgamesh
from the cold night wind, rested him on the ground,
encircled him with a sacred flour and hoped
that Gilgamesh could have a wishful dream.

With his chin resting on his knees, Gilgamesh went into
a normal sleep, but woke up confused.

Gilgamesh speaks to Enkidu:
    My friend Enkidu, I feel pain in my whole body,
    I feel stiffness in my arms and legs.
    Did you touch me and awaken me?
    Did a god pass by me?
    My friend, I had a second dream—a horrifying dream.
    I was seized by a mountain, it wrapped my legs
    and locked me up.
    I looked at the night sky and saw a shoot of light;
    it was a man with a face so bright.
    He freed me, he gave me water;
    his face filled my heart
    with trust and delight.

∾

Enkidu speaks to Gilgamesh:
    The man you saw was Shamash, your protector;
    the mountain that seized you was Humbaba.
    Shamash will never abandon you;
    he will cast his magical force on Humbaba
    and help us terminate him.

∾

After traveling one hundred and thirty-five miles,
they rested, fed themselves well, and resumed their trip.
After traveling one hundred and ninety-six miles,
they camped for the night; at the end of the day
they traveled three hundred and thirty-five miles.
In three days they traveled one thousand miles to reach
the outskirts of Mount Lebanon—a ninety-day journey
for a normal traveler.

At sunset, they dug a well near a mountain and filled
their water skins with fresh water.
Gilgamesh climbed the mountain, spread a sacred flour,

uplifted his head to heaven, faced the sun, and appealed
to Shamash to bestow upon him a pleasant dream.

At nighttime, Enkidu set up a tent to protect Gilgamesh
from the cold night wind, rested him on the ground,
encircled him with a sacred flour, and hoped
that Gilgamesh could have a wishful dream.
With his chin resting on his knees, Gilgamesh went into
a normal sleep, but woke up confused.

Gilgamesh speaks to Enkidu:
    My friend Enkidu, I feel pain in my whole body,
    I feel stiffness in my arms and legs.
    Did you touch me and awaken me?
    Did a god pass by me?
    My friend, I had another terrifying dream;
    it is as confusing as the other dreams.

    I saw a thundering cloud hovering above my head,
    and its echo shook my whole body.
    And suddenly, a fire engulfed the earth around me
    and then subsided.
    It turned everything into ashes
    as if death swept the land.

Enkidu speaks to Gilgamesh:
    My friend, the dream you had is a sign of hope.
    The thunder and the fire, the ashes that swept the land,
    is nothing but a battlefield in which we shall win.
    Nothing can stop our will to march into
    the Cedar Forest and to eradicate
    Humbaba from this earth.

After traveling one hundred and thirty-five miles,
they rested, fed themselves well, and resumed their trip.
After traveling one hundred and ninety-six miles,
they camped for the night; at the end of one day
they traveled three hundred and thirty-five miles.
In three days they traveled a close distance
of one thousand miles from Uruk to the outskirts
of Mount Lebanon—a ninety-day journey
for a normal traveler.

At sunset, they dug a well near a mountain and filled
their water skins with fresh water.
Gilgamesh climbed the mountain, spread a sacred flour,
uplifted his head to heaven, faced the sun, and appealed to Shamash
to bestow upon him a pleasant dream.

At nighttime, Enkidu set up a tent to protect Gilgamesh
from the cold night wind, rested him on the ground,
encircled him with a sacred flour, and hoped
that Gilgamesh could have a wishful dream.

With his chin resting on his knees, Gilgamesh went into
a normal sleep, but woke up confused.

Gilgamesh speaks to Enkidu:
    My friend Enkidu, I feel pain in my whole body,
    I feel stiffness in my arms and legs.
    Did you touch me and awaken me?
    Did a god pass by me?
    My friend, this dream I had aroused fear in me.
    I can't understand its revelation!

    I saw a terrifying bird with excessively large wings
    hovering above my head.
    When it breathed, it blew a blustery storm of death.
    When it opened its sharp beak, it spat fire!

A man suddenly appeared before me,
he captured the bird, broke his wings,
and severed his neck.

༄

Enkidu speaks to Gilgamesh:
　　My dear friend, my brother, the dream
　　you had was a hopeful dream.
　　The terrifying bird was evil Humbaba;
　　the man you saw was your protector Shamash.
　　He will protect us and grant us the will and the power
　　to win the battle against rancorous Humbaba.
　　Do not worry, my brother, as long as Shamash, the sun
　　god, is on our side!

After traveling one hundred and thirty-five miles,
they rested, fed themselves well, and resumed their trip.
After traveling one hundred and ninety-six miles,
they camped for the night; at the end of one day
they traveled three hundred and thirty-five miles.
In three days they traveled one thousand miles to reach
the outskirts of Mount Lebanon—a ninety-day journey
for a normal traveler.

At sunset, they dug a well near a mountain and filled
their water skins with fresh water.
Gilgamesh climbed the mountain, spread a sacred flour,
uplifted his head to heaven, faced the sun, and appealed
to Shamash to bestow upon him a pleasant dream.
At night, Enkidu set up a tent to protect Gilgamesh
from the cold night wind, rested him on the ground,
encircled him with a sacred flour, and hoped
that Gilgamesh could have a wishful dream.

With his chin resting on his knees, Gilgamesh went into
a normal sleep, but woke up confused.

Gilgamesh speaks to Enkidu:
>My friend Enkidu, I feel pain in my whole body,
>I feel stiffness in my arms and legs.
>Did you touch me and awaken me?
>Did a god pass by me?
>My friend, I had a dream unlike other dreams I had,
>and I hope it isn't an unfavorable indication!
>I saw a raging bull descending upon me,
>its hooves shook the earth,
>its thunderous roar blew clouds of dust;
>the dust was so dense, it changed daylight
>into total darkness.
>
>I tackled it and sat on my knees before it;
>I was breathless and helpless.
>
>A man came to my aid, picked me up,
>and set me on my feet.
>He gave me fresh water and cheered me.
>Tell me, my friend, if this dream is a sign
>of our downfall.

Enkidu speaks to Gilgamesh:
>My friend, do not be discouraged.
>The bull who descended upon you was the image
>of your guardian Shamash.
>He will lead us to the Cedar Forest and protect us
>from any act of evil;
>he will lead us back to Uruk safe and victorious.
>
>The man who picked you up and set you
>on your feet and gave you fresh water
>was your own father Lugalbanda.
>He will never abandon you and will be by your side

whenever you need him.
With this kind of help, we will accomplish things
no one ever dared to accomplish.

༄

When the two drew near the entrance to the Cedar Forest,
they heard a thunderous roar that shook the trees.
They knew that Humbaba was aware that someone
was trying to trespass his protected territory.
They were alarmed of the great danger they would face.

Enkidu speaks to Gilgamesh:
    My friend, I see tears filling your eyes,
    Are you afraid to go inside the Cedar Forest
    and fight Humbaba?
    You, my friend, beloved king of the great city of Uruk
    and its people, offspring of divine king Lugalbanda
    and lady wild cow Ninsun, should have the courage
    and the will to carry on our mission to kill Humbaba
    and to cut any cedar tree we want.
    You must put our destiny in the hands of
    your guardian Shamash.

༄

As he listened to Enkidu's encouragement,
Shamash's thunderous voice echoed in all directions.

Shamash speaks to Gilgamesh and Enkidu:
    Hurry up, get moving and enter the forest
    before Humbaba does.
    Humbaba possesses seven magical shields,
    and he is wearing one now.
    Do not give him the chance to use the other six,
    and when he does, he will be heavily protected

against any danger.
This is your chance to go inside the Cedar Forest
and attack him.

༄

The two friends could hear Humbaba's rage
from a distance.
His thunderous voice shook the forest,
and his footsteps shook the earth.

As he heard Humbaba's rage, Enkidu, too,
began to fear Humbaba; he was reluctant
to go inside the forest.

Enkidu speaks to Gilgamesh:
  My friend, attacking Humbaba could be a disaster,
  I know how vicious this creature is,
  and I know how tricky he is.
  I am worried about the two of us,
  but no matter what we stumble upon,
  we shall be together in this battle.

༄

Gilgamesh speaks to Enkidu:
  Do not be frightened, my friend.
  You have the heart of a warrior;
  he who fought beasts, fears no beasts.
  Settle down, strengthen your arms,
  and do not let defeat fret you.
  If life betrays us, valor will preserve us;
  he who is afraid of losing shall never deserve
  the glory of winning.
  Let us be courageous and march

inside the Cedar Forest and attack the beast;
he who leads protect himself
and safeguard his friend.

They drew closer to the entrance to the Cedar Forest
and decided to go together and challenge Humbaba.

Inscription V
THE DEATH OF HUMBABA

Walking near the entrance to the Cedar Forest and looking
at its vast stretch, the two friends were astonished
by its delightful view.
The forest was so dense with cedar trees of all sizes,
the leaves were so bright and so fresh, they filled the air
with pleasant sweet scent.
Cedar trees of all shapes and sizes, varieties of bushes and
brushes, were all in harmony with their natural setting.

The trail that led to the entrance to the Cedar Forest
bore traces of Humbaba's big footprints.
As the two friends reached the entrance to Cedar Forest, they caught
site of the holy mountain—
the abode of the gods and the goddesses—where the giant cedar trees
spread their shade
upon their dwelling.

Gilgamesh and Enkidu drew their swords and daggers
out of their scabbard, pulled their pickaxes
and hatchets out of their casing,
entered the sacred forest, and headed for the battle.

Enkidu speaks to Gilgamesh:
     My friend, be alert.

We are in the presence of danger!
 Humbaba is a merciless beast, he is sly and shrewd;
he might trick us and leads us into a trap.

∽

Gilgamesh speaks to Enkidu:
    My friend, there is no way back until we accomplish
    what we have planned.
    Fear not Humbaba,
    fear not his trickery,
    fear not his anger.
    Two men with willpower cannot be defeated easily;
    three-ply rope cannot be cut easily.
    Let us make use of our weapons and start the battle.

∽

The two friends entered the forest
with their heavy weapons.
They encouraged each other to be ready for the battle.
Humbaba, with his sharp hearing, detected
their movement, alerted himself, and stood offensively.
The two friends, as they neared him,
prepared themselves, and stood defensively.
Humbaba's roar exploded the air like a tornado.
It jolted the two warriors as if they were trees
falling by the force of a powerful winds.

Humbaba speaks to Gilgamesh:
    You, Gilgamesh, are fool to bring
    that inferior creature with you.
    You are fool if you listen to him.
    Who encouraged you to come to my forest
    and challenge me?
    Is it that son of a fish who led you to my forest?

I will crush both of you and
feed you to the scavengers.

∽

Humbaba speaks to Enkidu:
    You, Enkidu, son of a fish, no womb bore you,
    no father claimed you,
    no breast fed you;
    you are a son of terrestrial tortoise.

    I saw you when you were a tiny creature
    wandering in the wilderness among animals.
    I could have eaten you, but you couldn't even
    satisfy my appetite.
    Why do you bring Gilgamesh here
    to invade my forest and to attack me?
    I will wipe both of you from this earth,
    I will cut your throat, I will slice your flesh and feed it
    to the craws and let the scavengers finish both of you.

∽

Gilgamesh speaks to Enkidu:
    I fear Humbaba's temper.
    I see his face bursting with anger,
    and I am confused and worried. What shall we do?

∽

Enkidu speaks to Gilgamesh:
    My friend, you speak like a weak person.
    Do not let his intimidations frighten you.
    We will not abandon our mission.
    Let us go and fight him to the end.

Humbaba erupted like an earthquake.
When his feet crushed the ground, the earth shook,
Mount Lebanon shook; a heavy cloud of dust filled the air and fell
upon their heads.
They lost control of their movement,
and were knocked down to the ground—unaware what
had happened.

Shamash heard Humbaba's rage and became aware
of the danger the two friends are facing.
He struck Humbaba with shattering winds
from all directions: east wind, west wind, north wind,
south wind, gale wind, magical wind, and a blizzard.
Thirteen brutal winds struck Humbaba from all directions.
Humbaba stumbled and fell to the ground by the force of the brutal
winds.

Gilgamesh drew his weapons and pointed them at
Humbaba's neck; Humbaba knelt before Gilgamesh
and begged him for mercy.

Humbaba speaks to Gilgamesh:
    Gilgamesh, offspring of wild cow Ninsun,
    proud king of Uruk, descendent of monarchs,
    I beg you to offer me some mercy.
    Please let me live, and I will be your servant forever.
    I will cut for you all the trees you want,
    I will cut for you the holiest cedar tree.
    A dead man cannot fulfill his master's wish;
    so let me live and I will grant you all your wishes

Enkidu speaks to Gilgamesh:
    My dear friend, please listen to my advice.
    Do not believe in his promises,

he is sly and a liar, he will sneak on you;
kill him before he kills you.

⌒

Humbaba speaks to Enkidu:
You know well, Enkidu, the rules of the Cedar Forest.
Enlil placed me to guard this holy forest,
but you trespassed upon it.

Before you came into my forest,
I should have cut your throat and fed your flesh
to the crows and to all the scavengers.
If you don't tell Gilgamesh to save my life,
I will put a curse on both of you.

⌒

Enkidu speaks to Gilgamesh:
Gilgamesh, my friend, do not waste your time
listening to Humbaba's lies.
Kill him before it is too late.
Kill him before Enlil finds out.
Enlil in Nipur, Shamash in Larsa.
Kill him now.
Let the world and the people of Uruk know
who is the mightiest among all men.

⌒

Without hesitation, Gilgamesh drew his dagger
with one hand and his ax with the other.

He struck Humbaba in the neck with his ax, severed his head,
cut his abdomen with his dagger, pulled his intestine,
and cut his tongue.

Blood from Humbaba's body gushed in all directions.

Humbaba's blood, washed by the sliding rains from
Mount Lebanon, flooded the Cedar Forest.

Enkidu hauled Humbaba's severed head and saved it.
He wanted Gilgamesh to present it to the people of Uruk as a trophy.

Enkidu speaks to Gilgamesh:
    You, my friend, are the mightiest in the land.
    Now we can cherish the joy of our victory.
    Let us go and cut the tallest cedar tree in the forest;
    let us sail with it to Uruk to make a monumental door
    for Eanna's temple.

捣

The two friends assembled a raft and loaded
the cedar tree in it.
Enkidu took care of the navigation,
and Gilgamesh laid Humbaba's head on his side.
They let the current of the mighty Euphrates
glide the raft to Uruk.

Inscription VI
THE WAR OF WORDS WITH ISHTAR

Back in Uruk, Gilgamesh took off his blood-stained
clothes, washed himself well, shook his wet hair,
placed his tangled hair over his shoulder, and massaged
his body with herbal essence.
He dressed himself with the finest attire,
polished his blood-tainted weapons, tightened his regal
waistband, and set his royal crown on his head.

Ishtar, goddess of love, mesmerized
by his royal appearance, captivated
by his exceptional attractiveness,
tried to lure Gilgamesh to be her lover.

Ishtar speaks to Gilgamesh:
> Sweet Gilgamesh, feel me and make love to me,
> let me touch your gorgeous body, be my lover,
> be my husband, and I will promise you
> everything your heart desires.
>
> I will give you things no woman on earth
> can ever give you: a chariot of lapis lazuli and gold,
> its wheel shall be gold,
> its steering horns shall be bronze;
> thunder devils will drive it instead of mules.

Enter my house and marvel its cedar structure,
step on its cedar floor and watch how kings
and noblemen salute you and kneel before you
and offer you the pick of their harvest.

When you love me and dwell within me,
your goats shall give birth to triplets,
your ewes shall give birth to twins,
your donkeys shall outdo any mule,
your chariot horses shall outrun any horse,
your oxen shall outshine any bovine.

Be my husband, feel me, fondle me, make love to me
and I will give you everything I possess.

Gilgamesh speaks to Ishtar:
　　Do you want me to be your husband and lover?
　　Do you want me to satiate your sexual desire?
　　What can I give that you don't have?
　　Do you need clothing or scented oil for your body?
　　Do you need me to put ambrosia and beer
　　on your dining table?
　　You can have everything your heart desires,
　　but you can't have me as a husband or a lover!

　　You are a bed that can't warm up a lover,
　　you are a door that can't prevent the wind
　　from penetrating into its cracks,
　　you are a castle that collapses over its occupants,
　　you are an elephant that whips its own skin,
　　you are a load that breaks and burns
　　the hands of its bearer,
　　you are a water skin that seeps water
　　over his carrier,

you are a stone that can't hold a wall,
you are a shoe unfit to be worn!

What have you done to your lovers who gave you
the pleasure and the climax you desire?
You abused them when your desire was fulfilled!

Tummuz, who gave you the prime of his youth,
is now sighing from the agony you inflicted
upon him—a cycle of short life in the spring
and death in a long fall.

The singing nightingale, the bird you adored,
the bird you broke his wings, the bird you abandoned,
is now lying by the marshes crying "Ishtar broke my
wings, Ishtar broke my wings!"

The brave lion you loved and promised to care for,
is now entrapped in a pit. You incarcerated him in pits
after pits you dug to make his life worthless!

The fastest and strongest horse you loved is now
toiling nights and days, drinking muddy water
and suffering from the whipping you inflicted on him.
His mother Silili grieves everyday
at his intolerable condition.

The foremost shepherd you loved,
who baked fresh bread for you in a brick oven,
who slaughtered young lamb for you
and offered you its fresh-roasted meat to feast on,
is now a wolf who dares not to come near his herd.
What is your repay for his passion?
You turned him into a wolf and let his own dogs
bite him and chase him away from the herd.

Ishullanu, your father's gardener, who picked
a basketful of the freshest fruits and the sweetest dates
for you to garnish your table every day.
What is your repay for his passion?
You tried to seduce him to satisfy your sexual desire,
you tempted him to fondle you and get in you,
but he rejected all your temptations.
He refused to be disloyal to his mother, who fed him
the best food for life.
He refused to eat your food in shame or commit a sin;
he didn't want to be punished by sleeping
under a roof of reed unprotected by the rain and cold.
You made him a midget unable to have an erection!

My dear Ishtar, I don't want to turn my destiny into
a heartbreak suchlike your hapless lovers.

Ishtar could not hide her anger for long
when Gilgamesh insulted her.
With tears and anger, she ascended into the
seventh heaven complaining to her father Anu
and her mother Antu.

Ishtar speaks to her father, Anu:
    Dear father, Gilgamesh has insulted me
    for the way I have treated my ex-lovers.
    He rejected me, abused me, exposed my vices,
    and injured my feeling; I want to punish him for that.

Anu speaks to Ishtar:
    Dear daughter, your behavior let Gilgamesh
    expose your vices; for that reason

he rejected your advances.
You promised him things that he could not count on.

෮ඌ

Ishtar speaks to her father, Anu:
Please father, I want to punish Gilgamesh
for abusing me.
I want to have the Bull of Heaven gore Gilgamesh
to death for insulting me.
If you reject my plea, I will open the door
of the underworld and allow the dead to eat all the food
in the land and let the living starve to death.

෮ඌ

Anu speaks to Ishtar:
If I agree to your demand,
the Bull of Heaven will cause a destruction
all over the land.
The Bull of Heaven will dry the Euphrates River;
a famine will last for seven years.
The life of your people will be ruined!
Are you prepared for that?
Have you hoarded enough food for the people
and for their livestock?

෮ඌ

Ishtar speaks to her father, Anu:
Dear father, the people of Uruk have harvested enough
grain and feed to prevent a famine.
Yes, I have stored enough food to feed the people
and their livestock for seven years.

෮ඌ

Anu accepted Ishtar's demand and agreed to send her
the Bull of Heaven.
She led the Bull of Heaven by the nose ring,
descended with it to earth, and let it loose in Uruk.

His snort lowered the water in the Euphrates,
his rage caused a great fear among the people,
his stampede cracked the earth and blew the crops
in all directions and burned the reeds of the marshes.
His strong hoofs opened a deep pit, where one hundred
people fell to their death.
His strong hooves opened a second deep pit,
where two hundred people fell to their death.

His strong hooves opened a deeper pit, where Enkidu fell in,
but he jumped out and chased the bull.

Enkidu got the bull by its horns; the bull opened his mouth and spattered
thick saliva all over Enkidu's face.
Enkidu turned back and grabbed the bull by its tail;
the bull discharged a big dung all over Enkidu's body.

Enkidu speaks to Gilgamesh:
> Brother, the land and the crop is destroyed,
> and our people are dying.
> How can we answer our people?
> How can we show them our pride and might?
> We have to share the task: I will hold the bull
> by the tail, then you strike him with your sword
> in the upper neck.

∽

Enkidu chased the Bull of Heaven and got hold of his tail;
the bull tried to escape, but Enkidu overpowered him
and pulled him back.

With his sharp sword, Gilgamesh struck the bull
in the upper neck and killed him.
He cut the bull open and pulled out his heart.
Gilgamesh knelt before Shamash and gave him the bull's heart as a
sacrifice.
After killing the Bull of Heaven, Gilgamesh washed
his blood-stained body and went to rest.

Grieving over the death of the Bull of Heaven,
Ishtar stood above the wall of Uruk,
raised her hands, and began cursing Gilgamesh.
"You, Gilgamesh, have inflicted a great pain upon me."
she screamed. "May the god of the sky punish you
for killing the Bull of Heaven."

As he heard the curses against Gilgamesh,
Enkidu couldn't hide his emotion for long.
He cut a slab from the bull's thigh and threw it
on Ishtar's face.

Enkidu speaks to Ishtar:
> Let me catch you, Ishtar, and you will see
> how I will punish you!
> I will do unto you like I did unto the Bull of Heaven.
> I will handcuff you with his intestine.

Angry Ishtar went to Eanna's temple and prepared
a wailing session for the Bull of Heaven.
She ordered all the temple girls and the prostitute to
circle around the bull's thigh and mourn.

Gilgamesh invited the weapon's makers, the craftsmen,
and the smiths to see the massive size of the bull's horn.
They were stunned by its large size: each horn
weighed over 33 pounds in lapis lazuli,
each held 195 gallons of oil,

each had a thickness of two fingers.

Gilgamesh gave the horns to Lugalbanda, his father
and his guardian deity, to fill them with oil;
he hanged them in his sleeping room.

The two friends washed their hands in the Euphrates River,
hugged each other, held hands, and headed for
the streets of the great city of Uruk, where people
gathered to thank them and cheer them.

Gilgamesh gathered all the mistresses and the maids
of his palace and assembled a victory rally
to celebrate the killing of the Bull of Heaven.

Gilgamesh speaks to his household:
    Who is the greatest among men?
    Who is the most triumphant among heroes?
    Who is the king of all kings?

ᕬ

The household speaks to Gilgamesh:
    Gilgamesh is the strongest among men,
    Gilgamesh is the most triumphant among heroes,
    Gilgamesh is the king of all kings.

ᕬ

The parade ended cheerfully,
the victory rally concluded blissfully;
Gilgamesh felt relaxed and headed for bed.

Enkidu went into a deep sleep, and when he woke-up,
he told Gilgamesh about a terrifying dream he had.

Inscription VII
The curse

At the break of a new dawn, Enkidu woke up
and told Gilgamesh about a fearful dream
he saw during the night.

Enkidu speaks to Gilgamesh:
>My brother, my friend, the dream I saw last night
>worried me.
>I saw father of the gods Anu, god of the earth Enlil,
>god of the sweet water and the sea Ea, and sun
>god Shamash, assembled to impose
>a punishment upon us for the killing of the Bull of
>Heaven and Humbaba.
>
>I heard Anu saying to Enlil that the two of us are
>responsible for the killing of Humbaba,
>and one of us should die.
>But Enlil told Anu that I should die.
>I heard Shamash telling Enlil that the blessing
>and the protection he offered us encouraged us
>to invade the Cedar Forest and to kill Humbaba.
>Shamash also told Enlil that his safeguard helped us
>in the killing of the Bull of Heaven, and he demanded
>that I should not be blamed and should not die.
>Enlil rejected Shamash's demand and told him
>that I should die.
>My dear friend, my brother, I don't want to end up

in the netherworld sleeping with the dead.
I don't want anyone to separate me from you
and to prevent me from bearing my deep love for you.

❧

With tearful eyes and a mournful voice full of sorrow
and regret, Enkidu began to scream and swear
at the monumental door he built for the temple of Eanna.

Enkidu speaks to the cedar door:
    You, wooden slouch, empty of emotion,
    I know you can't thank me,
    I know you can't hear me.
    I searched sixty miles inside the Cedar Forest
    to find you fit as a door for the temple of Eanna.

No one ever built a door like you: thirty yards high,
eleven yards wide, fastened with rigid hinges
and shafts and joints and jambs—all perfectly fit on
twenty inches thick of the finest cedar wood on earth.
No one but the skillful craftsmen of Nipur can make
a massive door like you!

If I had known that your favor would be
a curse on me,
I would have raised my ax, cut you to pieces,
and made a raft out of you and set you adrift
over the Euphrates.

You, senseless door, after I leave this world,
may a king spit on you,
may he erase my name from you
and carve his name on you.

❧

Gilgamesh speaks to Enkidu:
> My friend, my brother, a curse cannot reverse a fate;
> fate is dictated by the gods.
> Do not feel sorry for your deed;
> sorrow is for actions people regret.
> Your dream was a good omen; all dreams, pleasant
> or unpleasant, are god given dreams!
> I shall plead to your god, to Shamash, and to
> all the gods to comfort you.

༁

By the early morning light, hopeless Enkidu aroused,
faced the sun, and appealed to Shamash.

Enkidu speaks to Shamash:
> I appeal to you, sun god Shamash, to prevent
> the trapper from catching any prey
> and from reaping any profit,
> I appeal to you to sadden his life
> as much as he saddened mine.
> I appeal to you to let him beg for muck to feed himself.
> He is the one who let Shamhat the prostitute
> seduce me and introduce me to the civilized world.

༁

Hopeless Enkidu did not stop cursing the trapper only,
but he also abused Shamhat mercilessly.

Enkidu speaks to Shamhat:
> Oh! Shamhat, may an everlasting curse
> befall upon you,
> may a rundown house, empty of children, board you,
> may all the men desire younger woman than you,
> may the drunks and the sobers vomit on you,

may the vomit smear your face and ruin your dress,
may the filthy street corners be your trading place,
may the dark shadow of the walls of Uruk
be your spot of trade,
may your breast and between your legs
be exposed to onlookers,
may an owl nest in your bedroom and hoot all night,
may the spiky thorns and the stinging shrubs
prick your feet.
You brought me into this civilized world, you little
harlot, and made me suffer from its aggravations!

ה

Sun god Shamash was displeased when he heard Enkidu
blaming Shamhat for his restlessness.

Shamash speaks to Enkidu:
Enkidu, why are you cursing Shamhat and accusing
her for seducing you and civilizing you?
Didn't she feed you bread and food proper
for the gods?
Didn't she offer you beer proper for kings?
Didn't she let you meet Gilgamesh, where you became
his brother and his best friend?

Gilgamesh will never abandon you;
he will have you rest in a bed of nobility,
and stretch you in a seat of royalty.
He will have you by his left side, where princes
of the netherworld kiss your feet;
he will have all the people of
Uruk pay their respects for you.
After you leave this world, Gilgamesh will
tear off his royal garment, dress himself
with a lion fur, throw his royal crown,

and have his hair matted.
After you leave this world, Gilgamesh will roam
the world in search for his own destiny,
in search for the secret of immortality,
in search of his ancestor Utanapishtim the faraway.

∾

Shamash advice and counsel subdued Enkidu's anger;
he became passionate toward Shamhat the harlot.

Enkidu speaks to Shamhat:
    I beseech the gods to bless you
    and to grant you the best thing in life.
    Rulers and men of power shall express their passion
    for you,
    young men shall have a climax three miles away
    from you,
    every male shall desire your body six miles away
    from you,
    soldiers shall strip naked before you and cover
    you with gold and silver and lapis lazuli,
    a man of wealth shall decorate your ears with
    golden earrings and your chest with
    lapis lazuli necklace.

∾

Lying alone in his bed, Enkidu experienced another
dreadful dream; he wanted to share it with Gilgamesh.

Enkidu speaks to Gilgamesh:
    My brother, my friend, I am disturbed about
    another dream I had.
    I was standing between a thundering heaven and
    a sweltering earth when I saw a terrifying creature.

His hands resemble a lion's hands with talon
like an eagle talon.
He pulled my hair and struck me to the ground,
I stood up on my feet and struck him back,
he subdued me and cuffed me and toppled me,
he changed me into a bird and dragged me
by the wings into a cavern of darkness,
where Irkalla rules; anyone who gets in to this place
of darkness can never get out.

I begged for your help, but you did not respond.
I saw dwellers of the cavern eat mud and grime,
I saw kings stripped of their crowns,
I saw rulers and kings serving cold water,
I saw them cooking and baking goods
in the dining halls of Anu and Enlil.

I saw ointment hands serving the great gods,
I saw high priests, minor priests, liturgy priests,
and recitals,
I saw Etana, the legendary king of Kish, and Samuqan,
god of cattle and wild animals.

I saw Belet-seri, scribe of the netherworld, bending
before Ereshkigal, ruler of the netherworld,
and reading words from a tablet held in her hands.
Belet-seri was surprised when she saw me,
and she asked herself why I was there.

❧

When Gilgamesh saw Enkidu bed-ridden,
he could not keep his emotion hidden.
He lowered his head and sighed;
he grieved and cried.

For twelve days and twelve nights, Enkidu's pain worsened,
he felt that his end was coming, and from his bedside
he wanted to tell Gilgamesh his regret
over his death in bed instead of a battlefield.

Enkidu speaks to Gilgamesh:
>My brother, my friend, I regret dying in my own bed.
>Why didn't I die as a warrior?
>I was avoiding battles, but now I wish
>I was dead in a battle!
>He who dies a warrior will die a hero's death;
>my death will be a death of an ordinary man.
>I want you, my friend, to stand by my bedside
>and listen to my sorrow.

At this instant, Gilgamesh felt that the end of his
dearest friend Enkidu was coming.

Inscription VIII
THE DEATH OF ENKIDU

Gilgamesh kept weeping by Enkidu's bedside
throughout a long night vigil.
The morning breeze and the bright sun
of an early morning could not cease Gilgamesh
from sobbing and sighing beside Enkidu's
motionless body.

Gilgamesh speaks to Enkidu:
 My dearest friend, my brother,
 the wilderness housed you,
 animals of the wilds loved you,
 the gazelle mothered you,
 the wild burro fathered you and raised you
 on donkey's milk,
 and I embraced you as a brother.

 Let the roads and the passageways to the Cedar Forest
 from sunrise to sunset grieve for you,
 let the people of the great city of Uruk sob for you,
 let the mountains and the hills, the meadows
 and the valleys weep for you,
 let the trees of the forests weep for you.

 Let the marshes hear the sobbing calls of our people.

Let the villages and the cities hear the sobbing roar
of the tigers and the lions,
of the leopards and the panthers,
of the bears and the hyenas,
and of the beasts of the jungles.
Let every town and every country hear the sobbing
of the deer, of the ibex and the bulls,
and of the grazing animals of the wild.

Let the divine river Ulay, where we walked along
its shores, bemoan you,
let the eternal river Euphrates, where we purified
ourselves and drank its water, bemoan you,
let the farmers, who sang blessing hymns
at our harvests, bemoan you,
let the shepherds, who gave you milk and butter,
bemoan you,
let the brewers, who let you drink the best of their ale,
bemoan you,
let the harlots, who conferred you with sensual
massages, shed tears for you,
let the newly wed and their guests
express their grief for you,
let the priests, the priestesses, and the harlots loosen
their braids for you.
My brother, my friend, let me weep for you!

Saddened by his friend's hopeless condition, Gilgamesh
expressed his rage like a loud thunder.
In a somber tone, Gilgamesh exposed his sadness
to the people of Uruk.

Gilgamesh speaks to the people of Uruk:
People of Uruk, young and old, hearken to my grief.
For the love of Enkidu I shall weep like

a yowling temple priestess,
for the love of Enkidu, the ax on my side,
the dagger in my scabbard, the spear in my hand,
shall curse the evil force who snatched him from me.

∽

Gilgamesh, sighing and crying, looking at
Enkidu's face and knowing
that his death is nearing.
Sitting by Enkidu's bedside, Gilgamesh recalled
the great times they had together—their intimate
friendship, their adventures and triumph,
and their love for each other.

Gilgamesh speaks to Enkidu:
　　My beloved Enkidu, you were faster than
　　a wild donkey,
　　swifter than a gazelle,
　　and stronger than a cheetah.
　　You were supreme against any force
　　that stood against you.

　　I shall cherish the time, the memories, and the
　　adventures we shared together: the parades,
　　the brotherhood, the feasts, the long and risky
　　journey to the Cedar Forest, the killing of rancorous
　　Humbaba, the killing of the Bull of Heaven,
　　and the celebrations of our victories.

　　Why the gods chose death for you?
　　What kind of sleep that took you away from me?
　　Why the faint light of the night
　　darkened your cheerful face?
　　I know you can't hear me.
　　I know you can't answer me.

~∽

Enkidu did not hear or answer Gilgamesh,
he did not lift his head or open his eyes;
his heart stopped beating.

Gilgamesh felt that Enkidu lost his battle,
and death defeated him.
He veiled Enkidu's face as if he was his bride,
he circled around his bed like an eagle
circling around its nest,
he paced the room back and forth
like a lioness guarding its cubs,
he ripped his clothing and dumped it
as if it was a curse,
he pulled part of his hair and threw it away in anger.

The night had dissipated under the birth of a new day,
but the new day did not alter Gilgamesh's
regretful mood.
His raucous voice could be heard all over the land.

Gilgamesh speaks to the people of Uruk:
      Craftsmen and metal sculptors,
      goldsmiths and gem cutters,
      cast for me a statue for Enkidu
      unparallel to any statue ever made.
      Cast its body with gold, lay its chest with lapis lazuli
      and its arms and legs with the most precious stones.

~∽

Gilgamesh speaks to Enkidu's motionless body:
      For you Enkidu, my brother, my friend, I will rest you
      in a place of nobility,

I will seat you in a chair of royalty,

I will lay you on my left side; monarchs and
noblemen and rulers of the netherworld
will lower their heads before you
and embrace your legs.

I will have the people of Uruk weep for you,
I will have every carefree shed tears for you.
And I, after your departure for the netherworld,
will let my hair wind below my shoulders.
I will wear a lion skin and wander
along the land and sea
in search for my own identity,
in search for the secret of eternity.

Gilgamesh realized that the only thing he could do
to reflect his love for Enkidu was to appeal to all the gods
for their blessings.
He went to his treasure chest and selected the best
he could offer the gods: gold, silver, ivory, carnelian,
lapis lazuli, and inlaid weapons.

He sacrificed an oxen and a sheep for his friend.
He placed all the offerings on a huge cedar table.
He filled a carnelian bowl with pure honey, lapis lazuli,
and pure butter and pleaded to sun god Shamash,
to moon god Sin, to the goddess of love Ishtar,
and to the ruler of the netherworld Ereshkigal to accept
the offering on behalf of Enkidu and to welcome him
in the netherworld as favorite dweller.

Inscription IX
THE LONG JOURNEY IN SEARCH OF IMMORTALITY

Gilgamesh looked at Enkidu's dead body
and began to question his own fate.

Gilgamesh speaks to himself:
    Death terrifies me!
    What becomes of me if I die?
    I don't want to end up like my dear friend Enkidu;
    I don't want to lay in a perpetual darkness
    of the netherworld.
    I want to live forever.

    I shall roam the world in search of immortality,
    I shall search for my ancestor Utanapishtim
    the faraway to seek his wisdom and his knowledge.

The sun dissipated beyond the horizon,
and a new moon lit the mountains and the valleys.
Resting under the moonlight near a mountain pass,
fearing the echoes of the roaring lions all night,
Gilgamesh faced the moon and appealed to
moon god Sin to safeguard him in the hours of darkness.

Gilgamesh speaks to the moon god, Sin:
> I appeal to you, moon god Sin,
> to protect me from the vicious lions,
> and from the ghostly creatures of the night.

❧

Deep in the night, Gilgamesh awoke from his sleep,
pulled his ax from his sheath and aimed it at
the roaring lions.
His ax traveled like a spear; it struck the lions
and knocked them dead.
He sliced their meat and ate it.

After a long and dangerous journey in a terrain
unfamiliar, Gilgamesh reached the site of
Mount Mashu, the twin peak mountain, where
its gateway leads into a tunnel where the sun
enters and sets, and exits and rises.
The twin peaks of Mount Mashu can reach
the seventh heaven,
and its base can reach the netherworld.

There were scorpion creatures—human from the waist up,
scorpion from the waist down—guarding the tunnel
where the sun sets and rises.
Their eerie looks are like a shock wave,
their semblance is like a tunnel of fear.
Their frightful look found no alarm in Gilgamesh.

The scorpion creatures stared at Gilgamesh intently,
Gilgamesh looked at them aggressively.
Feeling no fear, Gilgamesh went forth
and challenged them.

The scorpion creature speaks to his female companion:
    The man I see is not an ordinary man,
    he has the makeup of a divine man;
    his face bears a noble appeal.

⚬⚬

The scorpion creature speaks to her male companion:
    I can tell he is not an ordinary man.
    His face has all the marks of a king,
    his semblance has all the makeup of a divine man—
    two-thirds divine, one-third man.

⚬⚬

The male scorpion creature speaks to Gilgamesh:
    Godly man, who brought you to this no-man's-land?
    What provoked you to come to this faraway place?
    You must have the courage to cross a treacherous
    land and a turbulent sea where no man dared to cross.
    What motivated you to come here?

⚬⚬

Gilgamesh speaks to the male scorpion creature:
    I have lost a brother and a friend;
    his death depressed me
    and alarmed me about my own destiny.
    I am here searching for my ancestor Utanapishtim.
    Do you know the way to Utanapishtim the faraway?

⚬⚬

The male scorpion creature speaks to Gilgamesh:
    Godly man, no one can dare to cross the
    mammoth tunnel and come out alive.
    It stretches seventy-two miles,
    where absolute darkness entrenches it from

the rising of the sun to the setting of the sun.
You can't see anything in front of you or behind you.
You must exit the tunnel before the setting of the sun,
or you will be incinerated.

∞

Gilgamesh speaks to the male scorpion creature:
    With sorrow or pain,
    in full darkness or sunshine,
    I shall enter the gate.
    Open the gate for me,
    and let me cross the tunnel while it is dark.

∞

The scorpion creature speaks to her male companion:
    This man has the frame of mind and the willpower
    to defy any danger.
    He is self-assured and wise,
    and accepts no compromise.
    Open the gate for him, and let him
    cross the tunnel.

∞

The male scorpion creature speaks to Gilgamesh:
    Godly man, I will open the gate for you,
    and let you enter the tunnel with our blessing!
    May the tunnel's darkness lead you to
    a bright daylight,
    may your journey to the faraway land be safe,
    may your people celebrate your happy return
    with a grand reception.

∞

Gilgamesh entered the gate and ran through
the dark tunnel as fast as he could.

He traveled a distance of six miles in absolute darkness;
his eyes couldn't see what was in front of him
and what was behind him.
After traveling thirty more miles in absolute darkness,
Gilgamesh still couldn't see anything around him.
And after finishing forty-eight miles at a fast pace,
he still couldn't see the end of the tunnel.
After traveling six more miles, he felt a gentle breeze
refreshing his face.
After traveling another six miles in absolute darkness,
he was nearing the end of the tunnel; his eyes still
could not see anything in front of him or behind him.
It took him over seventy-two miles to reach the end of the
tunnel; he was in no danger to be incinerated by the sun.

When Gilgamesh reached the end of the tunnel,
he was captivated by the sight of an enchanting forest
that stretched wide and long before his eyes.
It bore the fruits of paradise: carnelian trees bearing
clusters of grapes, palm trees bearing golden dates,
fig trees bearing colossal figs, olive trees bearing
bright green olives.
He was bemused by the beauty of countless precious trees that
flooded the forest with brilliant reflections of light: lapis lazuli trees,
ruby trees, emerald trees, turquoise trees, and amber trees.

Gilgamesh spotted an inn by the seashore nearby.
He rushed to see if someone there could help him find
the way to Utanapishtim the faraway.

Inscription X
Discovering the passageway to
Utanapishtim's faraway land

Down by the seashore lives an innkeeper; Siduri is
her name—a wise and quick-witted matriarch.
A home-brewed ale from a golden barrel she serves
her patrons.
A veil she covers her body with.
A scarf she wraps her head with.

Sitting by her golden barrel, she saw a worn out man
wearing a lion skin coming her way.
His long hair dangled below his shoulders,
and he looked as if his strength was depleted from a long
and tiresome journey.

Frightened by the look of the man heading her way,
Siduri alerted herself and decided to protect herself.

Siduri the innkeeper speaks to herself:
    What does this man want from me?
    This man could not be trusted;
    he could be a murderer or a thief,
    and I should protect myself before it is too late.

೧ಲ

Siduri locked her gateway, bolted her door,
fled to the roof, and watched the wearied man
from the top of her inn.
Gilgamesh was outraged when he saw her hiding
on the roof.
He raised his head and screamed at her in anger.

Gilgamesh speaks to Siduri, the innkeeper:
　　Why did you shut the gateway when you saw me?
　　Why did you lock the door and flee to the roof?
　　I want you to open the gate and unlock the door
　　before I crash the gate and smash the door.

❦

Siduri speaks to Gilgamesh:
　　When I saw you coming near the gate,
　　I was terrified by the way you look!
　　I saw your cheeks so sunken,
　　I saw your face so pale,
　　I saw you so disgusted and frail.

　　Why is your skin frostbitten and sunburned?
　　You look like someone who came from
　　a long and exhausting journey.

❦

Gilgamesh speaks to Siduri, the innkeeper:
　　My name is Gilgamesh, king of the great city of Uruk.
　　Death has seized a dear friend and a faithful brother,
　　death has seized Enkidu, the love of my life.

　　Why shouldn't my cheeks be so sunken?
　　Why shouldn't my face be so pale?
　　Why shouldn't I be so disgusted and frail?

I crossed the barren desert under the scorching sun,
I crossed mountain passes and frozen terrains in search
of my own destiny.

Death has seized my daring friend Enkidu
who killed lions and hunted wild assess,
who roamed the wilderness with animals of the wild,
who ate with them and slept with them.

Side by side we invaded the Cedar Forest and killed
rancorous Humbaba,
side by side we cut the tallest cedar tree,
side by side we slaughtered the Bull of Heaven.
And now he is resting in the netherworld.

I cried for him days and nights,
six days and seven nights sorrow filled my heart,
six days and seven nights I refused to let his body
leave my place,
six days and seven nights I stood by his side until
a worm crawled out of his nose.

I don't want to end up like my dear friend Enkidu,
I don't want a worm to crawl out of my nose,
I don't want to end up in the cavernous netherworld.
I fear death.
I want to live forever.

৵

Siduri speaks to Gilgamesh:
Oh! Gilgamesh, what you seek you can never find.
Reality never turns unreal,
every human will face death,
and this is the commandment of the gods.
They direct your fate, and only the gods

plan their own destiny!

Enjoy life to the greatest limit,
go and blow your horn,
dance to the music and uplift your spirit,
you are created not to be reborn.
Make each day a feast,
take a pleasure in your food and fill your belly,
drink the best ale and be merry,
bathe in fresh water every day,
massage your body with scented oil
and herbal essence,
hug your children and make love to your wife,
enjoy the pleasure and accept the facts of life!
This is the way the human race ought to live.

∽

Gilgamesh speaks to Siduri, the innkeeper:
I am here searching for the secret of longevity,
I am here searching for my ancestor Utanapishtim
the faraway.
Tell me if you know the way.
Show me a pathway, a harbor or a waterway
that takes me to Utanapishtim the faraway.

Danger I fear not!
I will follow the most treacherous roads,
I will climb the highest mountain,
I will sail the most turbulent sea
until I get to my destiny.

∽

Siduri speaks to Gilgamesh:
Pay heed to my words, Gilgamesh.

There is a hazardous sea between you
and Utanapishtim; no one has ever crossed
the deadly water but Shamash the ablest!
In the middle of the sea, there are long miles
of Waters of Death to cross.
Are you willing to face this deadly water?

In the forest nearby dwells Urshanabi the ferryman
for Utanapishtim the faraway.
Seek him; he might help you.
You can find him in the forest
with his magical stones; they are his companion
who helps him avoid the danger
when he crosses the Waters of Death.

Ask if he can ferry you to Utanapishtim's dwelling.
If he can help you, take the voyage with him,
and if he can't, my advice to you is to head back home.

Gilgamesh, without hesitation, rushed to the forest.
He grabbed his ax from his belt, pulled his dagger
from his scabbard, and ran aggressively toward
the magical stones.
He smashed them to pieces and threw them into the river.
Urshanabi was outraged when he saw Gilgamesh
destroying his magical stones.
He tried to stop him, but failed.

Urshanabi, the ferryman, speaks to Gilgamesh:
I am Urshanabi, Utanapishtim's ferryman.

Who are you and where did you come from?
Who sent you here, and where are you going?
I am alarmed by the way you look!

I see your cheeks so sunken,
I see your face so pale,
you look so disgusted and frail.
Why is your skin frostbitten and sunburned?
You look like someone who came from
a long and exhausting journey.

❧

Gilgamesh speaks to Urshanabi, the ferryman:
My name is Gilgamesh, king of the great city of Uruk.
Death has seized a dear friend and a faithful brother,
death has seized Enkidu, the love of my life.
Why shouldn't I be grief-stricken?
I crossed the barren desert under the scorching sun,
I moved through the mountain passes and over
the frozen terrains in search of my own destiny.
I am here to find a way to reach Utanapishtim
my ancestor.
Could you show me the way
to meet Utanapishtim the faraway?

❧

Urshanabi, the ferryman, speaks to Gilgamesh:
Oh, Gilgamesh, your foolish act has deprived you
from sailing the dangerous sea.
You have smashed my companions,
the magical stones, and threw them into the river.
They do magic to protect me from the Waters of Death;
we will be in a great danger without them.

I request that you cut three hundred thrusting poles,
make each pole a hundred feet in length,
glaze them with tar, and cap their ends with metal.
If we try to use the thrusting poles properly,

we might cross the Waters of Death safely.

∽

Gilgamesh took his ax and went inside the forest,
cut three hundred poles, glazed them with tar,
capped their ends with metal, and loaded them
into the ferry boat.

They began their voyage encountering no threat until
they reached the edge of the Waters of Death.
It took them only three days to reach the edge of the Waters of Death
instead of forty-five day for other voyagers.
Urshanabi warned Gilgamesh about the danger
they would face.

Urshanabi, the ferryman, speaks to Gilgamesh:
    Get ready, Gilgamesh, to use a thrusting pole,
    be careful not to touch the Waters of Death,
    push carefully with a second, a third, and a fourth pole,
    push carefully with a fifth, a sixth, and a seventh pole,
    push carefully with the eleventh and the twelfth pole,
    and keep on using every pole until we come to the end
    of the deadly waters.

    Gilgamesh, we are safe now, the Waters of Death are
    behind us, and the passage to Utanapishtim
    is ahead of us.

∽

Urshanabi and Gilgamesh stripped off their clothing,
cut them to pieces, and used them as a sail.
Gilgamesh held the clothing with both hands and let the
wind glide them to the shores of Utanapishtim's dwelling.

As their ferryboat drew near the shores, Utanapishtim
became confused at what he saw aboard the ferryboat.

Utanapishtim speaks to himself:
    Where are the magical stones?
    Who is that man aboard the ferryboat with Urshanabi?
    That man is not one of mine,
    he looks tormented and weary,
    and I want to know who that man is and why he is
    coming to my shores.

∾

As soon as Gilgamesh's feet stepped on the shore land,
Utanapishtim began to question him.

Utanapishtim speaks to Gilgamesh:
    Who are you and what motivated you
    to come to my shores?
    Your face reflects a man who came from
    a long and dreadful journey.
    I see your cheeks so sunken,
    I see your face so pale,
    You look disgusted and frail!
    I see your skin frostbitten and sunburned.

∾

Gilgamesh speaks to Utanapishtim:
    My name is Gilgamesh, king of the great city of Uruk.
    Death has seized a dear friend and a faithful brother,
    death has seized Enkidu, the love of my life.
    Why shouldn't I be grief-stricken?
    I crossed the barren desert under the scorching sun,
    I moved through the mountain passes and over

the frozen terrains in search of my own destiny.

Death has seized my daring friend Enkidu
who killed lions and hunted wild asses,
who roamed the wilderness with animals of the wild,
who ate with them and slept with them.

Side by side we invaded the Cedar Forest and killed
rancorous Humbaba,
side by side we slaughtered the Bull of Heaven.
My dearest friend Enkidu is resting now
in the netherworld.

I cried for him days and nights.
Six days and seven nights I declined to let his body
leave my place,
six days and seven nights I stood by his side until
a worm crawled out of his nose.

I don't want to end up like my dear friend Enkidu,
I don't want a worm crawling out of my nose,
I don't want to end up in the cavernous netherworld.
I fear death!
Death frightens me!
Yes, I came from a long and a dire journey
in search of immortality,
in search for Utanapishtim the faraway.

Utanapishtim speaks to Gilgamesh:
Gilgamesh, I am Utanapishtim of Shuruppak,
son of Ubar-Tutu.
I survived the great flood
and joined the assembly of the gods
who granted me an eternal life.

Gilgamesh, you are the son of divine king Lugalbanda,
offspring of cow goddess Ninsun, by virtue of whom
you are two-thirds divine, one-third man.
The gods gave you the command to be a king.
Why is your heart agitated with sorrow?
Look at your life, give it a serious thought,
weigh it against the feeble
who eat spoiled butter instead of fresh butter,
who eat tainted bread instead of freshly baked bread,
who eat wheat husk instead of wheat flour,
who wear knee shorts to cover their organs
instead of decent clothing to cover their whole body!

Life is as fragile as a thin, dry reed,
and death is unpredictable and has no mercy
on humankind.
Death can deprive the offspring
from reaching maturity;
it can strike any age at any time and place.
No house is built to last forever,
no deeds or laws last forever,
no brothers outdo their inheritance,
no river can flood the land forever.

When the butterfly leaves her larva and sees the sun,
oftentimes it breaks her wings and dies.
Death is an inhabitable island, yet not trespassed upon;
it is a nebulous place suspended
between night and day,
it is a dealing with reality and accepting possibilities.

Gilgamesh, you have to accept the facts of life and
be satisfied with what you are and what you have.
Why do you deliver a part of you to death?
Because Enkidu is irreplaceable, and that part is
beyond your comprehension.

One calls into the sleeper, one addresses the sleeper
into his grief!
One feels his own death—the dizzying nothingness
relentless of answers!
Gilgamesh, take care of the heart that lives in despair,
for it is life that betrays it.

When the Anunnaki, gods of judgment, hold their
caucus with Mammitum, gods of destiny,
they plan the fate of humankind,
and they dictate the time of life
and the time of death,
but they reveal life and conceal death.

Inscription XI
THE STORY OF THE GREAT FLOOD

Gilgamesh was astonished when he met Utanapishtim.
He envisioned Utanapishtim as a godlike being.
But when he looked at him,
he saw all the traits of an ordinary man in him.

Gilgamesh speaks to Utanapishtim:
> I am looking at you, immortal man, and see
> all the traits of an ordinary man in you.
> I first thought of you as a warrior ready for altercation.
> I was ready to confront you, but now I am eager to
> acquire knowledge and wisdom from you.
> Why are you "the chosen?"
> Why did the gods choose you among other
> humans and grant you immortality?

Utanapishtim speaks to Gilgamesh:
> I will tell you, Gilgamesh, why I was "the chosen,"
> and how the gods granted me immortality.
> I will tell you a secret only the gods know,
> but I will reveal that secret to you.

On the bank of the river Euphrates was

a city named Shuruppak—a city well known to you.
Time had decayed that city; the gods who lived there
became so old and helpless.
The assembly of the gods decided to destroy
and exterminate its inhabitants.
No guilt in their heart, the assembly of the gods
had decided to create the Great Flood to eradicate
humanity and to destroy everything in its path.

The assembly of the gods congregated
with the father of the gods Anu,
with their arbitrator brave god Enlil,
with their steward partisan god Ninurta,
and with their overseers Ennugi, to settle on a plan
to destroy every living thing.
They all agreed on a decision to generate
a destructive flood, but they kept it a secret.

Wise god Ea was also present at the congregation.
He revealed the secret to the house of reed.
He faced the house of reed and spoke through
its walls, saying:
"Oh! Walls, tell the house of reed to hearken to me.
Oh! King of Shuruppak, son of Ubar-Tutu,
raze your house and leave behind all your possessions,
leave behind your city,
save your life and build a ship,
set its dimensions equal in height and width,
put a roof on top of it to save the ship from
outpouring water,
gather on board every living creature you can find,
and escape with your life and everything you possess."

I was seized by the words of advice from wise god Ea!
I acknowledged his advice, but was hesitant
to let my people know.

"Tell me, my savior," I said, "what shall I tell
my people?"
Wise god Ea advised me to tell my people
that Enlil holds an extreme hostility against me,
that I can't live anymore within his boundary,
that I should move with wise god Ea in his place
under the sea,
that wise god Ea will bless them with
plentiful rain and bountiful harvest,
that he will let the clouds rain
the best fish and fowl upon them,
that he will let the heavens drop wheat
and fresh-baked bread for them.

I told my people that they should be grateful for
the blessing wise god Ea promised them to deliver
after my departure.

Ea's advice and warning made me think seriously
about building a ship according to his specifications
to escape the destructive flood.

Early in the morning I gathered the young and the old
around me and began a plan to build the ship.
The children carried buckets of caulking tar,
the elders and the weak carried the lightweight loads,
the carpenters and the craftsmen brought their tools,
and everyone worked days and nights doing the task
according to their skills and performance.

Five days had passed and the ship frame
was completely assembled.
One acre I made its floor space,
eight hundred and forty-eight thousand cubic feet
I made its interior space—enough to hold
everything I gathered.

The workforce implemented my plan by dividing
the ship interior into six levels; they added a seventh
level over the deck, and divided each level
into nine chambers.

We plugged all the holes and joints with wedges
and sealed them with caulking tar,
we poured a thousand buckets of tar into the furnace,
we used thirty thousand buckets of asphalt
to seal the ship.

Thirty thousand buckets of oil were moved
by young helpers into the ship,
ten thousand buckets were used for soaking the poles,
twenty thousand buckets were saved in the storage
compartment by the ship pilot.

Lamb and beef I fed my working men,
sheep I slaughtered for them every day,
wine and beer I served them every night;
they drank it like water gushing from a flooded river.
They fared their time drinking and singing
as it was a new year's eve celebration!
And after seven days of hard work, the ship was
completely built.
I soothed my hands with scented oil and took a rest.
On that day, before sunset, the ship was ready
to be drawn into the water,
but we encountered some difficulties.
We drove long rods under the ship and rolled
it into the water until two-thirds of it submerged.

At the dawn of a new day, as the sun rose above
the horizon, my family, the ship workers, men of
skills, craftsmen, and artisans went on board.
I secured all my possessions inside the ship, and let all

the animals I gathered move into the ship.

"When you see a massive, dense cloud cover the
bright morning sun," sun god Shamash warned me,
"you should gather all your belongings and rush to the
ship and seal all its doors."

Before sunset, I looked at the sky—dark and dreary!
I saw the rain pouring faster than a flooded river,
I rushed to the ship with all my belongings,
I sealed all the doors and gave command
to Puzur-Amurri to pilot my ship.

I was vigilant throughout the night,
and by the rising of the early morning sun,
I saw deep, dark clouds charging from the far horizon.
I saw Adad, god of thunder and storm,
steering the clouds, and ahead of him, riding over
the mountain and the lowland, were the messengers
of the storm, Shullat and Hanish.

Nergal broke the water barriers,
Ninurta opened the protective dam and let the deep
water pour like a violent cyclone,
the Anunnaki lit their torches and set the land ablaze.
Adad blasted a thundering storm that turned the daylight
into a complete darkness; nothing was visible
to the eyes, and no one could recognize his family
or see anything around him.

The thundering storm was so powerful,
it cracked the earth.
Water from the sky and the rivers sank buildings and
forests and reached as high as a mountain!
A powerful south wind blew violently all day
and swept everything in its path like an invading army.

Even the gods were frightened by the destruction
caused by the Great Flood; they escaped to
Anu's seventh heaven.
Crouching against heaven's wall, shivering like wet
dogs, the gods begged Anu to open his heaven's gate.

Even goddess Ishtar felt the suffering caused by the
Great Flood; she cried like a pregnant woman in labor!
And with her pleasant voice, she uttered evil words at
the assembly of the gods, and blamed them for the
destruction they inflicted upon her people
and their land.
"Nothing left from the olden days but dust," Ishtar told
the assembly of the gods, "my city is destroyed,
my people have vanished from this land. I blessed their
lives, and now they are like dead fish
drifting over the shores."

The Anunnaki felt the suffering too.
They lowered their heads and cried;
sealed their lips and heaved a sigh.
For six days and seven nights, the water swept the land
from all directions, and created an enormous flood—
destroying every living thing in its path.

On the seventh day, the destructive storm
started to calm down,
the flood water began to recede,
and a notable silence prevailed over the land.
I opened a vent and felt the puff of a cool air
and the warmth of an early morning sun upon my face.

I looked outside at different directions
and saw how the flood caused all that destruction.
It flattened everything in its path; leaving the land
like a stretch of a barren desert.

I couldn't believe my eyes when I saw people
turned into clay.
Tears flooded my eyes; I lowered my head
in deep sorrow.

The boat was stranded when it struck the
edge of Mount Nimush—it kept it
aground for six days.

On the seventh day,
I freed a dove,
it couldn't find a place to land,
it returned back to the boat.

I freed a swallow,
it couldn't find a place to land,
it returned back to the boat.
I freed a raven,
It found a place to land and things to feed on,
it didn't return back to the boat.
Then I freed everything on board the ship
in all directions and offered a sacrifice
for the four winds.

I poured holy water on the peak of the mountain
for a blessing,
I set-up fourteen pots on the side of the mountain
and lit sugar cane, cedar, and myrtle in the pot holes.
The gods smelled the sweet-scented air; they rushed to
the site and gathered around the pots like flies!

At the gathering came mother goddess Aruru
bursting with anger.
She exposed her breast and displayed the lapis lazuli
necklace Anu had given her in admiration.
And Aruru said, "Hear me, O god, I shall never

detach this lapis lazuli necklace from my breast, I shall
never forget the olden days, I shall never forget my
people and their land. Let all the gods be at this
gathering except Enlil, who caused the Great Flood
and the destruction of my people and their land."

Enlil suddenly appeared at the gathering of the gods.
When he saw me aboard the ship, he became
so enraged at the Igigi gods.
He blamed them for revealing the secret to me.
He was stunned when he saw me alive; he thought that
the destructive flood had eradicated all humankind.

Because Ea knew the intent of the flood, Ninurta also
suspected him for revealing its secret to me.

But Ninurta accused Enlil for the enormous damage
the flood caused without weighing its consequences.
He told Enlil that he should have let every human
pay for his sin, every wrongdoer pay for
his wrongdoing, and anyone who is accused
without reason shall not be worthy of punishment.
In addition, Ninurta also expressed a deep emotion
toward Enlil.
He told him that he could have done other things
to punish humankind, that he could have lions or
wolves, a plague or a famine to punish them.

Ea denied telling the intention of the flood to me.
He told the assembly of the gods that he only talked to
the house of reed and revealed the secret of the flood
to its wall; Utanapishtim heard the echo from
the wall in his dream.

At the end, Enlil took me by the hands into the ship,
brought my wife aboard, stood between us, made us

kneel before him, and blessed us.
And by a declaration from the assembly of the gods,
Enlil granted me and my wife an eternal life.
He proclaimed that we are chosen to be gods like him,
and assigned us a faraway dwelling by the river source.

My dear Gilgamesh, this was the story of
the Great Flood, and how and why the gods granted us
immortality and secured us this faraway dwelling.

ᕲᕰ

So impressed by the astonishing story of the survival
of the Great Flood, Gilgamesh appealed to Utanapishtim
the faraway to find him a way to overcome death.

Utanapishtim speaks to Gilgamesh:
Gilgamesh, be that as it may,
who will sanction the assembly of the gods for you?
who will persuade the gods to grant you an eternal life?
In order for the gods to listen to your plea, you must
fulfill a task—you must be awake for six days
and seven nights.

ᕲᕰ

Gilgamesh sat down, relaxed and rested his
chin on his knees,
but he was subdued by a deep sleep
like that of a midnight cloud seizing a golden moon.

Utanapishtim speaks to his wife:
Come and see how this demanding man
betrays his own self.
Look at the way he slept, disregarding his wish!

How could we trust a man who gave up
his own determination?

๑๏

The wife speaks to Utanapishtim:
Wake him up, rest him on his back, and help him
go to his homeland safe.

๑๏

Utanapishtim speaks to his wife:
Deception is an inherent trait of humankind!
Do not let this man deceive you.
Let us put him to the test while he is asleep.
I want you bake a piece of flat bread for each day
he sleeps, place each piece by his side, count the days
in which he sleeps, and mark them on the wall.

๑๏

As Gilgamesh kept on sleeping, Utanapishtim's wife
kept on baking flat bread each day he was asleep,
put it by his side, and marked the day on the wall.

The first piece of bread crumbled like a broken pot,
the second gathered mold,
the third became like a sheep skin,
the crust of the fourth turned white and reaped mildew,
the fifth started to rot,
but the sixth one kept its freshness.
And when the seventh piece was still on the griddle,
Gilgamesh woke up from a patting on his back.

Gilgamesh speaks to Utanapishtim:
I was too tired;

I was unaware of what had happened to me.
My eyes felt heavy,
my whole body felt motionless,
and suddenly a nap took over me.
I don't know what to do, and I want you to help me.

◯◯

Utanapishtim speaks to Gilgamesh:
It wasn't a nap you have taken;
it was a deep sleep for six days and seven nights.
Look at the marking on the wall.
look at the bread that sets by your side: the first piece
crumbled like a broken pot,
the second developed mold,
the third became like a sheep skin,
the crust of the fourth turned white with mildew,
the fifth started to rot,
but the sixth kept its freshness.
And when I awakened you, the seventh piece was still
baking on the griddle.

You have failed the test, and I can't help you anymore.
Be truthful to yourself and prepare to go back
to your homeland.

◯◯

Gilgamesh speaks to Utanapishtim:
I am lost in this world of mine
and don't know what to do.
I am lost between reality and delusion, and whatever
I do, my thoughts on life and death terrify me.

◯◯

Utanapishtim speaks to Urshanabi, the ferryman:
    My ferryman, I condemn the foolish handling
    of your duty.
    I shall never see you set foot on my shores.
    Take this man to his homeland clean and safe,
    and never come back to my shores again.

    Go and care for this distressed man,
    ask him what he needs,
    take him to the wellspring and wash his tangled hair,
    unwrap his beautiful body from that animal skin,
    let the sea waves carry the wastes away,
    rub his body with scented oil,
    fit him with an outfit suited for a king,
    and leave with him to his homeland decorous and neat.

                    ᘒ

The ferryman led Gilgamesh to the wellspring,
washed his tangled hair,
unwrapped the animal skin that marred his body,
and let the sea waves carry it away.
He rubbed Gilgamesh's body with scented oil,
dressed him with an outfit proper for a king,
decorated his head with a royal crown.

Urshanabi boarded the ferryboat with Gilgamesh,
and began to depart.

The wife speaks to Utanapishtim:
    That man faced all kinds of danger
    and felt all types of pain to reach our shores.
    Please don't let him go home empty-handed.
    See what you can offer him to take back home.

                    ᘒ

Utanapishtim speaks to Gilgamesh:
    Your journey to this faraway land has caused you
    a considerable distress and hardship.
    I shall not let you go to your homeland empty-handed.
    I shall reveal to you a secret only the gods know.
    There is a thorny herbal plant at the bottom of the sea;
    be careful of its sharp thorns.
    This plant has a supernatural power;
    it will bring back youth to old age;
    it will rejuvenate anyone who eats it.
    I will show you where it is located.

As soon as Gilgamesh heard that,
he opened a passageway,
wrapped a heavy stone to his feet,
and dived down all the way to the bottom of the sea
where the plant is located

Gilgamesh pulled the plant with both hands,
regardless of the pain the thorns inflicted upon him,
cut off the stone from his feet and pulled himself
up to the surface.

Gilgamesh speaks to Urshanabi:
    I have in my hands a plant that will bring back
    youth to old age, and I shall call it the herb of youth.
    I will test it on my people;
    if it works, I will use it myself.
    Let us head for home blessed with what we have.

After traveling sixty miles, they stopped for food.
After traveling ninety miles, they rested for the night.

At daytime, Gilgamesh decided to bathe in a cool lagoon nearby.
He put aside the herbal plant and jumped into the water.
A snake smelled it from a distant, came closer, sniffed it, and ate it.
It sloughed its skin and rejuvenated its life.

Saddened by the lost of the herbal plant,
Gilgamesh realized that all he hopes for is gone.
He felt so depressed—he screeched, then wept.

Gilgamesh speaks to Urshanabi:
    Why did a snake rob everything I hoped for?
    My hopes are gone,
    my search reaped naught,
    my toil left me empty-handed,
    and I can't bear the pain of despair.

    I can't go back to search for the herbal plant,
    I don't remember its location,
    I have no marks to lead me,
    no tools to work with,
    and nothing can help me.

ᢏᢢ

After traveling sixty miles, they stopped for food.
After traveling ninety miles,
they felt tired and rested for the night.

It took them a long and exhausting journey
to reach the outskirts of the great city of Uruk.

Gilgamesh looked at the walls of the city he loved
and felt highly spirited and fortunate.
With a sigh of relief, Gilgamesh finally acknowledged
his lifelong achievement.

Gilgamesh speaks to Urshanabi:
    Look at the wall of my beloved Uruk.
    Examine its splendor and observe its structure—fire-
    hardened bricks laid by the hands of the Seven Sages.
    Every brick sparkles like bright copper.
    Nothing like it ever was!

    Step on the threshold and enter the gate,
    climb the stairways and walk on top of the wall,
    look bellow and see Uruk's brilliant plan:
    three and a half miles its expanse,
    one square mile its city dwellings,
    one square mile its date palms and fruit farm,
    one square mile its meadows.
    Nothing like it ever was!

    Step down and enter Eanna's temple,
    move inside its one-half mile stretch
    and marvel its stunning structure.
    nothing like it ever was!

About the Author

After graduating from high school in Baghdad, Iraq, Sam Kuraishi came to the United States as a student.

He first enrolled in an accelerated program at the English Language Institute of the University of Michigan. After completing the program, he attended East Tennessee State University, where he earned a Bachelor of Science degree in mathematics and a minor in English and industrial art. He enrolled in graduate classes at the Illinois Institute of Technology, where he studied printmaking and kinetic sculpture.

Kuraishi worked for advertising agencies and publishers as a designer of advertising materials and books. He also taught the subjects at a local college in Chicago.

He finished all the qualifications for a master's degree in the development of human resources.

Reading Jack Kerouac's book *On the Road* and the poems of Allen Ginsburg, Laurence Ferlighetti, Leroy Jones, and other Beat generation writers and poets, Kuraishi developed a passion for their work. He was also inspired by the work of Carl Sandburg and the Chicago Circle writers: Studs Terkel and Nelson Algren and their contemporaries.

Some of his work was published by *The Great Lakes Review,* a literary journal on American Midwest culture. He published a local magazine for over five years, for which he interviewed many local and international personalities.

He lives in the Chicago area with his wife, Betool, and divides his time between writing, working on digital graphic projects, and relishing the work of Walt Whitman, William Carlos Williams, and Khalil Gibran.

6391177R00090

Made in the USA
San Bernardino, CA
07 December 2013